Metaverse for Beginners

An Ideal Guide for Beginners to Understanding and Invest in the Metaverse: NFT Non-Fungible Token, Virtual Land, Real Estate, Defi, Blockchain Gaming and Web 3.0

Darell Freeman
Cryptosphere Academy

Disclaimer

All the information in this book is to be used for informational and educational purposes only. The author will not, in any way, account for any results that stem from the use of the contents herein. While conscious and creative attempts have been made to ensure that all information provided herein is as accurate and helpful as possible, the author is not legally bound to be responsible for any damage caused by the accuracy and the use/misuse of this information.

TABLET OF CONTENTS

INTRODUCTION

In the future of the Internet, there will be virtual worlds where humans can interact without the limitations of physical space. Welcome to the age of the Metaverse. According to analysts' predictions, these virtual environments could be the next big investment opportunity.

Technology companies can develop virtual environments thanks to increased computing power, faster Internet connections, and technological advances in artificial intelligence and machine learning. These spaces are intended to give participants the feeling of being there without having to leave their seats. As Meta CEO Mark Zuckerberg explained in a recent video, Meta is committed to providing people with the opportunity to "do almost anything you can imagine" using holograms driven by virtual reality arrays and other devices.

In this future world, people will be able to teleport as avatars into virtual environments and digitally experience most of their daily activities, including work, play, shopping, exercise, and learning. They can also recreate real-life spaces, such as the interiors of their homes and offices, as well as sophisticated graphic representations, such as the beaches of Hawaii. As Meta says, the virtual is idealized when imagination and reality mix.

In a Metaverse meeting," Zuckerberg explains, "you don't just see a grid of faces on a screen, you have the feeling of being in a room together, of eye contact, of a shared space. This feeling is common to all experiences in the virtual world. For example, a teacher can take students to ancient Rome or the depths of the Amazon jungle through augmented reality, an augmented version of the real world.

CHAPTER 1: Insight into investing in virtual Real Estate, including the buy and flip approach and huddling

Over the past few decades, Internet technology has revolutionized the way we experience the world, giving us unrestricted access to information and expanding our social interactions. The next evolution, however, is likely to be more immersive technology.

Digital real estate is being deployed on virtual platforms such as Decentraland and OpenSea. Both are places on the Internet where consumers can buy and sell digital products such as music, art, fashion products, and now real products as well.

For many people, the concept of valuing things in the digital world is still new. You may wonder what use there is for real assets that are not tangible.

The first thing to understand is that as the Metaverse develops, the user will begin to establish an identity within it (similar to avatars in video games). Just as avatars need clothes to wear, they also need places to visit in the Metaverse. This is where digital properties come into play.

What Is The Metaverse?

Since Facebook announced its entry into the Metaverse, awareness of this new space has been overwhelmingly positive. Everyone has heard the term "Metaverse" on the Internet, but because of its "newness," few people actually understand how it works.

The Metaverse is best described as an alternative digital reality where users go to work, engage in leisure, and host digital identities. It combines elements of virtual reality and augmented reality to simulate real-world experiences, and is essentially the latest Internet. (It is also often referred to as Web 3.0).

The term "Metaverse" itself has been around for a long time. However, it has recently gained popularity because of the business opportunities created by Facebook's announcement.

One of those business opportunities is actually the buying and selling of digital real estate. These virtual lands are the meeting places for our digital identities (avatars). This is because as more and more users enter the Metaverse, the need for digital real estate is expected to increase.

It seems like a very simple thing to do. Buy a house, make some cosmetic changes, put it on the market again, and get a big profit. There are always six TV shows with good-looking, well-dressed investors making the process look fast, fun, and profitable.

In addition, several residences are being flipped. Flipping homes accounted for 6.2 percent of all home sales in the United States in 2019, according to data revealed in a report by ATTOM Data Solutions. This is the highest percentage in eight years. Reports that are speculative A little dip occurred in 2020, but the numbers began to rise again in the second quarter of the following year, 2021.

However, the road to real estate wealth is not all about curbs and "sold" signs. Many people who aspire to become real estate kings ignore the basics and fail. So what are the five biggest mistakes that aspiring real estate speculators make, and how can you avoid them?

Speculating in real estate is just like any other business. It takes knowledge, planning, and skill to succeed.

The most common mistake novice real estate investors make is to underestimate the time and money required for the project.

Another mistake that real estate speculators make is to overestimate their skills and knowledge.

In a time-based business like real estate investing, patience and good judgment are especially important.

How Real Estate Speculation Works

Real estate speculation (also known as wholesale real estate investment) is a real estate investment strategy in which an investor buys real estate, but does not use it, and then sells it for a profit.

Speculative investors focus on the purchase and subsequent resale of a property or group of properties. Many investors try to generate a steady income by flipping properties frequently.

So how do you flip a building or a house? The simple answer is to buy low and sell high (just like any other investment). But instead of a buy-and-hold strategy, close the deal as quickly as possible to reduce the time your money is exposed to risk. In general, the emphasis is on speed, not on maximum profit. This is because every day that goes by costs money (mortgage, utilities, property taxes, insurance, and other expenses associated with home ownership). This is a common plan, although there are some pitfalls.

These benefits are usually brought about by price appreciation when the real estate market is strong and prices rise sharply, or by capital improvements to the property, or both. For example, an investor can buy an existing home in a trendy neighborhood, make extensive renovations, and then sell it at a price that reflects the new look and amenities.

Why investors are paying real money for virtual land

Chris Adamo is proud to say that he started investing in NFTs (Non-Fungible Token) late; he got his first one in the summer of 2021. But when it comes to buying real estate in the metaspace, Adamo is ahead of the curve: eight months ago, the Miami-based venture capitalist and a group of partners calling themselves MetaCollective DAO used the virtual real estate brokerage to buy 23 parcels in a user-created, blockchain-based virtual blockchain-based virtual world "Sandbox" for as little as 1 ETH (about $3,000). One property in the neighborhood sold for about 42 ETH, or $130,000.

This land (Pixel) is adjacent to the site of the Bowling Monkeys Yacht Club in downtown NFT and land owned by Adidas. We call it Sandbox Hill Road, after Sandbox, the famous Silicon Valley platform where this "land" is located. The value of these parcels has increased tenfold and their possessions could be worth millions of dollars.

"It's like the New York of sandboxes," Adamo said. Now it's like the Lower East Side or Soho. Translation, it's a fad, or at least they claim to believe it is possible.

If Metaverse is a virtual entity that includes everything from digital art to virtual worlds, then the real estate parcels discussed here can be considered a type of Metaverse investment and are often classified as NFTs. These virtual worlds - The Sandbox, Decentraland, Cryptovoxels, Earth2, Nifty Island, Superworld, and Wilder World - offer something different to users in terms of surrealistic graphics, gameplay options, and early adopter communities. All of them offer something different to the user. (For example, Snoop Dogg builds his own house in Sandbox and Paris Hilton has an island in Roblox.)

If you open Sandbox in a web browser now, all you see is a flat map with brand logos scattered over a terrain made of colored pixels (each pixel or parcel is a highly valuable asset. On the Internet, the concept of scarcity is generally a sham, but in this world it tends to be as real as in the physical world). In cryptovoxels, on the other hand, it is more like a video game.Cryptovoxels, on the other hand, has the feel of an early stage video game, with pure white dolls walking around (Click on the poster for more information about NFT's work and artists, and a link to OpenSea, NFT's marketplace).

The MetaCollective has big plans for this blank rectangle. For Drew Austin, managing partner of venture capital syndicate RedBeard Ventures and head of MetaCollective, it's about turning this corner of the Internet of the future into a learning center or "university" for self-education in all things Web3. For Drew Austin, who heads MetaCollective, the idea is to develop this corner of the Internet of the future into a learning center or "university" for self-education in all things Web3. It envisions virtual classrooms, dormitories that users can rent, and a full social experience. "What a digital educational experience is," he says, "we can recreate in this new digital world. None of this has been constructed or developed as of this writing.But the money is real.

One could think of it as buying a domain name or getting a good name on social media. If email is home for each of us on Web 1, and social profiles like Facebook and Instagram on Web 2, personal property in the form of virtual real estate could be the Web version of Web 3. The difference is that you, the end user, can build that experience yourself, rather than relying on a vendor or platform. For brands, it can be much more interactive and active than your current digital presence. For individuals, it means playing games and selling products to generate revenue.

Andrew Steinwold, managing partner of the native Metaverse fund Sfermion, calls this "infinite optionality," free from the confines of profiles and pages. A whole industry of virtual world developers is already in place. The beauty of the Metaverse is that it's a co-creation," says Jessica Pelz Zatulove, a member of the Meta Collective. It's a fusion of creator, celebrity and community. For the time being, though, all of this is pure supposition

The big winners, at least for now, are the platforms and the creators, who are attracting investment capital from early buyers: Animoca Brands, which runs The Sandbox, recently reported a valuation of $5 billion, up from just over $2 billion in 2021. Roblox, a more established game universe, went public in New York in March 2021 with a valuation of $42 billion. A research report predicts that the virtual gaming universe alone could be worth $400 billion by 2025, and that the Metaverse industry as a whole will be worth more than $1 trillion.

His optimism is ultimately self-serving, as many first-time buyers of virtual real estate are dually invested in the platform itself and through personal games like DAO, where they buy and develop new land (Steinwold's fund, for example, makes investments in both platforms and personal property, while Austin runs a fund that invests in five different worlds). Austin also points out that there is a lot of "room for improvement," from the interface to the technically complex process of buying a property.

However, Web3 investors are very interested in the service: according to CNBC, the price of virtual property has gone up 500% since Facebook switched to Meta. Some virtual world plots are already as expensive as real world homes.

The gateway to Decentraland, a 3D virtual world platform where Uy.ser can buy virtual plots on the platform as NFTs via the cryptocurrency MANA, a sidechain of Ethereum. It will open to the public in February 2020 and is overseen by the non-profit foundation Decentraland.

But while the casual user experience leaves much to be desired, the ways to claim land and real estate development plans are expanding every day: ONE Sotheby's has just announced that it will build virtual replicas of real-world properties in The Sandbox and cross-ownership. Meanwhile, there's an anonymous buyer who bought the land next to Snoop Dogg for $450,000, perhaps banking on the added value of proximity to a famous neighbor in the same way that MetaCollective is banking on the

Bored Ape Yacht Club; at Cryptovoxels, a developer is planning to build a New York Stock Exchange-style trading center and headquarters for cryptocurrency companies like defi protocols in the heart of Frankfurt. The dream is that this place will become the central hub of this world, something that will really help us as we move into the virtual world.

This may sound far-fetched, and rightly so. Investors, too, are skeptical of the virtual world today; Steinwold, who has raised more than $100 million from investors for his fund, sees much of the virtual world speculation so far as overvalued. In fact, he says, Web3's overvaluation is "across the board," from NFT art to crypto tokens. However, this hasn't deterred him from making investments at the "level of developing a firm" thus far and it hasn't stopped them from supporting the Frankfurt NYSE plan with cryptovoxels." It's like the days before Napster. There's no Napster yet, there's no iTunes, there's no Spotify," he says, likening the current virtual world to the music-sharing platforms of the early 2000s and their successors." It will come, but it will take a long time."

For Zatruv, another investor in Metacore, the appeal lies in the business potential. As a founding partner of Hannah Grey, an early-stage venture firm focused on the potential of new platforms for brands, Zatruv is focused on finding ways to integrate commerce into this new landscape." You have an office in a prime location, but the real question is, "Can we rent this land?" and "Can we have a store? Can we host events? This is the moment of the virtual real estate gold rush. People don't know what they're going to build or how they're going to build, but they're buying land in the best places to create interesting economic futures." She imagines setting up an office on Metacore's campus.

"Maybe we could have a coffee shop or a cool place. We could have meetings with the city council, office hours for the founders, and a museum to inspire creativity through collaboration between the different architects who live in this space," she brainstorms. Moreover, the market is untapped. Zaturov cited the fact that there are 3 billion gamers in the world and they are accustomed to spending time in virtual environments. The appeal of virtual real estate is that you find yourself creating your own opportunities," he said.

Adamo has children and, like any parent, is thinking about their future. This property may not be an actual store, but it was still purchased with their best interests in mind." Looking at this year's growth rate, it really seems to be a multi-generational planned purchase. Perhaps Sandbox Hill Road will disappear into the Internet ether in a few years, like Limewire and Kazaa. Maybe we've bought the Spotify of the future. Meanwhile, the bubble is only getting bigger.

Why invest in virtual land or real estate?

Land sells for a lot of money" is probably one of the most exaggerated clichés we've all heard.

If you could get a dollar for every time you heard this cliché, the Forbes list would be overcrowded.

The cliché of skyrocketing land prices resonates both from the sales talk of real estate agents and when people are confused about their investment choices, including real estate and asset holdings.

Interestingly, the emergence of digital assets is changing the dynamics of the real estate market and presenting us with a more complex dilemma. Virtual land in the Metaverse or real land in the universe?

One weekend on Twitter Spaces (a feature of Twitter that allows users to discuss various topics in a forum-like setting) talking about non-fungible tokens (NFTs) and cryptocurrency.

The speakers on this channel talked about the rise of NFTs and how African content creators can leverage digital resources such as NFTs and virtual reality. With all this talk, people become curious about the prospects for NFT and the Metaverse (a concept we've heard of but still don't understand).

The speakers were asked, "Two million dollars of virtual land or two million dollars of banana island land?”

Most people bought the $2 million virtual land because of its futuristic valuation, which may exceed the original $2 million. The speaker who chose the equivalent of a banana island was interested in the "entity" because the present was more important to him than the future.

Can we say that the discussion of Virtual Land and Real Island is about comparing the future with the present? Or exponential versus arithmetic evaluation?

Has this changed your mind about seeing a virtual $2 million piece of land as a better investment property than a house on a banana island? Perhaps we can borrow one of the hidden golden rules of the real estate market. Land is valued. Houses are depreciable.

Real estate investment is about buying properties that will increase in value over time, providing capital growth and good returns. If the Metaverse can do that, then so much the better. Can't we look at other factors? Virtual land will not be taxed due to its "decentralization," but the owner of a banana island will pay some sort of property tax.

Many of us missed the first bus with cryptocurrencies, do we want to make the same mistake with the Metaverse and NFT?

Investors who are bullish on the upside of the Metaverse are investing heavily in the companies building it, Meta (Facebook), Microsoft, Nvidia, Unity and Roblox. They have also invested in the cryptocurrencies that are building the Metaverse, Axie Infinity, Decentraland (Mana), The Sandbox and Theta.

The evangelists of the Metaverse tell us that we will be able to buy and sell clothes, cars, cannabis, and socialize in this virtual world. But let's ignore this illusion. Aren't we doing these things in the real world as well? What is the metaphor of underdeveloped countries suffering from energy shortages, is reality?

This is why a $2 million property on Banana Island is, for some, a no-brainer. Years of work and effort should bring "substantial" rewards. Banana Island is a millionaire's paradise, with royal, wealthy and prosperous neighbors, and access to the best resources and facilities. That is the ceiling for the rich in Nigeria, but again - ceilings must be broken, so we still have the option of Metaverse. it will be interesting to see the world 10 years from now. Maybe the COVID will have mutated to the 475th species and we will have no choice but to live in the Metaverse or Elon Musk's Mars colony. We'll just have to go with the flow till then.

What is the ROI of digital real estate?

Depending on the land use, there are many opportunities for digital real estate investors. Virtual land is bought and sold in cryptocurrency, so those with experience in crypto trading have an advantage.

Investors can buy land in the Metaverse and build whatever they want, whether it's a performance venue to host music events or a co-working space to hold business meetings.

To give you a concrete example, Snoop Dogg is currently developing a "Snoopverse" on Sandbox, a virtual reality platform for gaming and entertainment; Snoopverse refers to Snoop Dogg's own virtual world within the Metaverse. Earlier this month, a fan calling himself P-Ape bought a digital section of the Snoopverse for $450,000.

I'm always looking for new ways to connect with my fans, and what we've created with The Sandbox is the future of virtual meet-ups, NFT drops and limited edition concerts," the rapper and entrepreneur said of his latest endeavor.

Although intangible, ownership in the Metaverse can certainly be profitable. In June of this year, a piece of land sold for over $900,000 on

Decentraland, one of the most popular platforms for buying digital real estate. The transaction took place in the cryptocurrency, (MANA), a sidechain of Ethereum.

Another notable digital real estate transaction that took place in the Metaverse this year was Tokens.com's $2.8 million purchase of virtual land in the nearby Fashion District, as the origins of NFT and VR lie in the gaming world, where users began buying clothes for their avatars. Fashion is a particularly promising industry in the Metaverse.

There are several virtual worlds where one can start investing. For investors interested in real estate, Decentraland is undoubtedly the most popular. As of this week, the lowest price for land on Decentraland is 3,087 Ether, which is equivalent to $13,675.

How to buy land in the Metaverse

Get a digital wallet

You can't buy digital real estate with real dollars. You need cryptocurrency. The first step is to create a digital wallet so that you can buy virtual land with the appropriate currencies. (This is similar to exchanging dollars for reals when you go to Brazil, or yen for reals when you go to China.)

In Decentraland, this currency is known as MANA. In the Sandbox, where Snoop's Snoopverse is hosted, the currency is known as SAND - you need MANA to buy land in Decentraland and SAND to buy land in the Sandbox. These two currencies are not interchangeable.

Regardless of which currency you choose, be sure to take note of the seed phrase you are given when you open your wallet. Think of this as your "virtual bank account" information. Keep it handy and memorize it if you can. Seed phrases are very difficult to get back once you lose them.

Next, buy SAND or ETH on Binance and transfer it to your wallet.

To buy or bid on land, you need SAND or Ether (ETH) in your portfolio. You can purchase SAND or ETH using your credit or debit card in your Binance account

Once you have purchased the crypto, you need to transfer it to your crypto wallet. Copy the public address of your cryptocurrency wallet and use it as your withdrawal address. Step 2: Select a Buying Platform

Once you have your digital wallet set up, you have a few choices when it comes to buying land: you can buy real estate directly on a Metaverse platform like Decentraland or Sandbox, or you can buy via a third-party platform like OpenSea. The choice is yours.

For first time investors, it may be best to look at third party platforms; OpenSea and NonFungible.com allow you to compare virtual plots without having to constantly jump from one platform to another. Different platforms have different buyers' price ranges and digital plotting services. It is tedious to jump from multiple platforms during onshore evaluation.

Third-party platforms also allow purchasers to evaluate the selling price in terms of the actual local currency, making it easier to see how much is actually being spent on a particular investment. This is especially important given that each cryptocurrency has its own value, independent of other currencies.

The advantage of buying land directly within a Metaverse platform like Decentraland or Sandbox is that you have a strong sense of what products are available there and who your neighbors are. This is probably the most advantageous route to take after gaining some experience as a digital real estate investor.

Choose a buying platform

You can easily categorize the available land parcels in sandBox and use the following filters to make an offer or purchase Most of the land in sandBox has already been purchased, so you will usually only find available land on OpenSea You can buy land through the Sandbox map. However, it is possible to bid on these sales through the Sandbox map. The Sandbox map is also a great way to check if you are buying a legitimate NFT plot, as it has an OpenSea link embedded in its user interface.

Once you find a plot you want to buy, you can either click the [Bid] button to make an offer, or click on the ETH amount to buy it at a fixed price. Now let's click [Bid] and see how to place a bid.

A pop-up window to place a bid will appear. Enter your bid amount, click [Bid], and then confirm the transaction in your wallet. If the seller rejects your bid or the sale is closed, the cryptocurrency will be returned to your wallet.

Clicking on the fixed price will take you to OpenSea, where you can complete the transaction. Before buying land, you need to link your wallet to the market. You can also use OpenSea to make an offer if you do not want to go through The Sandbox.

Make an offer & close on your virtual real estate

In the real world, closing on a property may be the hardest part. In digital real estate, this is not the case, at least not yet. Once you find the land you want to buy, all you have to do is click and buy.

There are no appraisals in the Metaverse, at least for the time being. However, there is the possibility of price negotiation. For example, Decentraland allows you to make an offer and the owner can accept or reject it.

Once the portfolio is funded, the package is selected, and the price is set, you are ready to buy. The transaction will be recorded in your portfolio and will generate an NFT title to your unique property.

A few considerations...

You need to keep in mind that the Metaverse is uncharted territory. Digital real estate investing is an extremely new form of investing and it is changing rapidly.

A few months ago, you could own a piece of digital real estate for a few hundred dollars; entering 2021, you need a few thousand for a start

There is not enough transaction history of digital real estate transactions to determine how the virtual real estate market will work. Investing in it is highly speculative and the market is currently in a volatile state.

We are not hesitant to invest in digital real estate and it is important to note that there are no price tolerances or demand level determinations for these new assets. Be mindful of the amount of money you allocate to this new venture.

Should you buy and hold real estate or flip properties?

There is no right answer to the question of whether buying and holding real estate is the best strategy for real estate investment. Rather, choosing one method over the other should be part of a clear strategic plan that takes into account your overall goals.

The opportunities presented by existing markets should also be considered. Here is a description of each strategy and how to determine which strategy is right for you.

1. Flipping real estate and buying/owning real estate are two different investment strategies.

2. Real estate ownership provides investors with the opportunity to avoid the ups and downs of the stock market and accumulate wealth over time.

3. Flipping offers a faster return on investment and always avoids the hassles of finding tenants and maintaining the property, but the costs and taxes can be high.

4. Buying and holding real estate provides a passive monthly income and tax benefits,

but not everyone is prepared for the management and legal responsibilities of being a landlord

Buy and hold or flip: which strategy is right for you

You've just bought a new property and haven't decided what you want to do with it. Should you make a quick profit and move on, or should you think about staying with it for the long haul? Here are some questions to ask yourself to help you decide which strategy is right for you.

1. What is my investment objective?

First, you need to determine your objectives.

Fix and Flip Real Estate Investor

A fix and flip real estate investor aims to get their hands on a property, fix it up as quickly as possible, and sell it at a profit. This way, carrying costs are lowered and a larger profit can be earned.

Buy And Hold Real Estate For Investor

Buy-and-hold investors choose to hold properties as leases in order to generate cash flow. Even though they may not make much profit initially, they are able to generate income from the property over a longer period of time than fixed and reverse investors.

2. Are the benefits greater than the risks?

The fix and flip investor

The fix-and-flip method offers a single large return for the investor, and the money is immediately returned to the investor's pocket. Because the fix and flip is done in a relatively short period of time, the investor is not exposed to the long-term value fluctuations of the normal market.

However, flippers need to keep their cool when making financial decisions about a property. They must make sure that they do not overpay or underpay for the property.

Buy And Hold Investors

Buying and holding real estate is a proven, long-term strategy that can help accumulate wealth and ensure long-term income flow. Even if the value of real estate declines for a period of time, it has been established that most real estate values will increase over time, so buy-and-hold investors are holding valuable assets and accumulating wealth if they are willing to wait for market fluctuations.

The biggest risks for buy-and-hold investors are bad tenants and bad property managers. Finding good tenants takes time and patience, which is a full-time job in itself for a new property owner. Keeping good tenants and getting rid of bad tenants is also a difficult situation.

Remember to consider the following considerations before making your selection.

1. Fix and flip investors.

Investors need to realistically fix the cost of the project over time and anticipate unexpected expenses. In the flipping business, time is money. Delays can dramatically increase costs and decrease profits due to extra months of maintenance costs such as loan payments, property taxes, insurance, utilities, lawn care, and snow removal.

In some areas, a certain sale price is mandatory, no matter what modifications have been made. To gain wealth from residential investments, there are a number of investors who either have not improved their properties enough to sell them, even at market price, or who have over-improved their properties in hopes of selling for much more than the local market price.

Finally, television shows about buying and selling homes make it sound so easy that anyone can do it, but nothing could be further from the truth. No one should enter the real estate investment business without understanding how best to structure their flipping deals, what the tax implications could be, or the myriad of risks associated with starting a business based on speculative values. Investing in flipping houses is not for everyone, so new flippers should start with very small properties and ensure that they have the skill and temperament for this process.

2. Buy and hold investors

Many buy and hold property investors do not have the skills to be property managers and will need to learn the process (and the relevant landlord and tenant laws) quickly or hire an outside property management company. A good property management company is well worth the cost, but a bad property management company is time consuming, expensive, and can reduce the value of your investment. Needless to say, a bad property management company or a bad tenant can damage your property, cause extra costs, and reduce your cash flow.

Don't get caught up in one strategy or the other

Many investors who work with Rehab Financial Group both rotate for immediate income and buy and hold for long-term real estate investments. They balance their portfolios in the same way that others balance their financial investments, such as stocks, bonds, and mutual funds.

In both scenarios, real estate investors need to be clear about their own goals and their financial capacity to deal with market downturns, unforeseen costs, and tax implications.

Two ways to flip a property

There are two ways to flip a property.

1. Buy a property in a growing market and hold it for a short period of time, only to resell it at a higher price.

2. Buy a property below market value, make minor renovations, and strategically refurbish the property so that it can be sold at or above market value.

Pros and cons of flipping

It is important to know the pros and cons of flipping a property before you start. As with any high-risk investment, there are great rewards if everything goes according to plan, and potentially horrible mistakes if your plans go awry. Here are some things to consider

Pros Of Flipping A Property

Flipping a property can be extremely rewarding. Here are just a few of the advantages.

1. Make a quick profit

One of the biggest reasons people go into a property reversion is to make a quick buck. If done correctly, ownership flips can bring in very large profits, often exceeding the average annual salary in the US.These returns can be achieved in a very short period of time, often in just a few months.

You can gain insight into construction by repairing, renovating and remodeling properties.You will gain an understanding of the costs of materials and various repairs, such as plumbing and electrical. You will learn how to spot larger problems, such as structural issues and environmental hazards like mold and asbestos.

You will also learn how to budget for unexpected costs, such as

1. Building permits

2. Delays in construction and delivery of materials

3. Disputes between contractors

4. Maintenance costs if a property does not sell as quickly as expected

By gaining this construction experience, you will know how to budget optimally for a business and make more profits on future projects.

5. Understanding the local market

Before you actually buy a property, you should always do some market research. You should talk to real estate agents in the area, look at the 'for sale' ads, and see the homes that have recently sold.

In this way, you should be able to get a good sense of what people are looking for in the region. A modern design may be popular in one part of the country, while a traditional design is another winner.

This is why you should always do your research and target your renovations to your local market.

6. Developing the buyer's insight

Once you have put your first flipped property on the market, you will have an even deeper insight into what buyers in the area are looking for. By taking these notes, you can make the necessary adjustments to your next flip, hopefully with even more success.

Flipping properties is a great way to increase your knowledge about the real estate industry in general. Whether you are a first-time shortsale buyer or a foreclosure buyer, we will walk you through the process and the various financing and refinancing options available to you.

7. Increase your network

While doing this, you can make a lot of new industry contacts, such as;

- Real estate agents
- Lawyers
- Contractors
- Building inspectors
- Insurance brokers and other investors

These contacts can also be useful when working on future investments and personal assets.

8. Personal achievement

Another benefit of moving real estate is that you get to know the potential of a property that others may not see as much. Having the vision to create value in a home is a source of great personal achievement, along with the ability to achieve financial returns that are far superior to most other types of investments that are available to the common investor.

The Cons Of Real Estate Flipping

Along with the benefits of real estate resale, there are also risks. Here are some of the drawbacks of flipping real estate.

1. Risk of loss

The biggest problem with flipping is when the flip becomes a flop and you lose money. There are many factors that contribute to this loss, including

2. Unexpected expenses

These include everything from building permits and contractor delays to unbudgeted renovations and material costs. These costs can quickly pile up and eat away at potential profits. They can also force the seller to make concessions to the buyer, and these concessions can also contribute to the bottom line.

3. Tax Increases

Once the renovation is complete, the city may raise your property taxes. Buyers may have a hard time finding a buyer and have to pay the taxes themselves, or the higher taxes may affect buyers who may reconsider purchasing the property.

4. Capital Gains Tax

Profits from investment properties may be subject to capital gains tax, and the capital gains tax rate varies depending on whether the property has been owned for less than or more than one year.

It is also possible to do a 1031-Exchange and defer the tax to a future point in time.

5. Maintenance Costs

The longer you own the property, the more you will lose.

Even after the renovation of the property is completed, you will still have to pay the mortgage (assuming the property is mortgaged), taxes, and insurance premiums for as long as you own the property.

You may also have to pay additional maintenance costs such as yard maintenance and snow removal. Also, the longer a property is on the market, the more likely it is that the price will have to be lowered, eating up any anticipated profit.

6. Stress

Stress is also a drawback of real estate rehabilitation. Some of the causes of stress can include the following

7. Finding the best property

8. Proper estimation of necessary costs

9. Dealing with contractors, real estate agents, and local ordinances

10. Trying to meet deadlines

11. Finding a potential buyer

Knowing the pros and cons of flipping so you can make an informed investment

Pros and cons of buy and hold

There are basically two ways to invest in stocks. You can either go too fast and take big risks, or you can do it the safe and stable way. While many investors prefer the former to earn huge income in a short period of time, there are a few who prefer the latter. These are the long-term investors.

Long-term investors invest with the motto of buying low and selling high. They search the market to find undervalued stocks and invest in them with the intention of holding them for months or years. They usually do their research based on the fundamentals and good management of the company, and who wouldn't want to own Reliance Industries today at 1990s prices? This buy and hold is a risk-free investment.

This buy-and-hold is also a low-risk investment strategy, but there are many pros and cons associated with it. It is important to know them in detail before implementing this strategy. Let's get right into the details of the main pros and cons of this buy and hold strategy.

Pros Of A Passive Buy And Hold Strategy

Let's take a detailed look at some of the advantages and pros of the passive buy-and-hold strategy.

1. Less hassle

Most investors prefer the buy and hold strategy because it is almost hassle-free compared to short-term investments and intraday trading. All you have to do is select stocks based on fundamental analysis and invest a portion of your capital. All you have to do is wait for the price to rise and you have a high probability of closing your position and extracting a profit. You don't have to stay glued to the screen all day and place frequent trade orders. However, solid fundamental analysis is necessary for successful investing, and Market Neuron can help you choose between 6 and 10 stocks to buy and hold based on your fundamental analysis.

It works. It has been proven over time that this investment strategy works most of the time, which is why it is considered a safer investment option compared to intraday or short-term investments. However, a proper analysis of a company's fundamentals is required before investing. Thus, all you have to do is choose a stock with strong fundamentals, invest your money and wait.

2. It's Based on Cold Hard Facts

Fundamental analysis involves a deep analysis of the company's knowledge. This knowledge is usually solid facts that are notable in nature and are not manipulated. Therefore, as long as you have had a basic analysis from the experts, there is a very limited chance of having a wrong decision.

3. Great for tax purposes

Last but not least, the tax incurred on long-term capital gains is lower compared to short-term capital gains: positions held for more than a year are considered long-term investments and are taxed at a more favorable rate.

Cons Of Passive Buying And Holding

There are a number of disadvantages to the buy and hold strategy. This section discusses the disadvantages of passive buy and hold strategies.

1. Capital lockup

A buy and hold passive strategy requires that you have capital invested for a long investment period, which means that you will not have access to capital for several months or years. This means that you will not have access to your capital for several months or years. In an emergency, you may have to liquidate your position at a loss because you sold earlier than anticipated.

2. Tiat

This is clearly a time-consuming strategy. You may have to invest for months or years, and the stocks you choose may not show the expected movement and end up underperforming. In that case, the returns will be lower than expected.

3. Market crashes

Holding a position for 10 years does not necessarily mean that the stock price is infallible. There are many factors contributing to market crashes that are beyond the scope of your planning. The recent outbreak of the Covid 19 pandemic is one such example.

Buy and hold is one of the most favored investment strategies in the market. Investors who implement this strategy do not have to worry about market timing. Nor do they have to base their decisions on subjective analysis. However, it should be noted that, like all other investment strategies, the buy and hold strategy carries a number of associated risks. Therefore, it is advisable to obtain an analysis of your risk profile from a recognized investment advisor before investing.

Choosing A Strategy

If you want to become a real estate investor, the first step is to decide which real estate investment strategy is right for you. Buy and hold or buy and flip?

Both strategies have the potential to be profitable, but only one is suitable for your skill set, financial situation and goals.

Ultimately, neither strategy is better than the other. The question is which one is better suited to your skillset and financial situation and which one will help you achieve your goals.

If you are looking for a way to passively grow your assets over a long period of time, with low risk and requiring little time, then buy and hold may be a better choice.

If you are looking for a more aggressive investment and want to see a quick return, then buy and flip is the way to go. However, this option is riskier, so before you take the plunge, you need to make sure you have the skills and knowledge to make it happen.

Fixing And Flipping The Investment

First of all, let's discuss fixing and flipping. The fix and flip strategy, if executed correctly, is to purchase a property at a price below market value, improve the property through strategic rehabilitation, and then sell that same property for a financial gain. This strategy has received a lot of attention and in my opinion, may be a more glamorous option compared to buy and hold. This is partly due to the fact that repairs and modifications have been brought into the limelight by HGTV's 12-

hour long "Flip This House" broadcast. While the short-term profits may be attractive, this investment strategy is not for everyone. Flip houses require a number of skills, strategies, and risk tolerance.

1. Get-Rich-Quick Upside

The relatively short turnaround and large profit margins associated with fixed and flipping investment strategies definitely attracts people. There are few other investment opportunities that have the same economic upside as house flipping. For example, some investors have doubled their investment capital in just a few months. While doubling is not the norm, the ability to earn high returns in a short period of time will be more attractive to many investors than buy and hold, which requires waiting for years.

2. Speed Is Of The Essence

When flipping houses, one of the biggest factors in profitability is time. A good investor needs to get into the house quickly and get out of the house quickly. The longer the holding period, the more carrying costs they will have to pay, which will eat into their profits. These costs include monthly bills that accumulate over time, such as utilities, property taxes, HOA fees (if applicable), finance charges, and other maintenance costs.

3. The "Fix" In Fix And Flip.

This may sound like a simple task, but it involves asking yourself, "Can I fix this property? A large part of your profit will come from being able to predict the cost of repairs and complete them within your budget. If you are able to do the work yourself, you will save a lot of money. If you do not have the personal skills, it is imperative that you have strong relationships with local builders and tradesmen. Investors with construction experience often have an advantage when it comes to property rehabilitation.

4. Understand Your Taxes

Short-term capital gains from flipping real estate can result in higher taxes in the near term compared to long-term investments. A fix-and-flip investor does not enjoy the same tax benefits as a buy-and-hold investor. Therefore, they need to better understand the tax implications and factor them into their projections and business plans in order to accurately predict profits.

Buy And Hold Investing

Moving to buy-and-hold - This strategy is quite different from a fix-and-flip because the investor buys a home to hold for the long term (no immediate exit strategy). This is usually done by purchasing an asset, fixing up the property as needed, and then renting it out to tenants for a monthly fee. With this strategy, investors can profit in two ways: through the monthly cash flow generated from renting and through the long-term appreciation of the asset. Buy-and-hold is known as an excellent way to accumulate wealth and generate continuous cash flow.

1. Slow Wealth Accumulation

Whereas fix and flip is all about speed and making a profit quickly, buy and hold is a turtle's pace. It doesn't start fast, but it eventually creates great wealth and liquidity. The secret of this turtle is simple. In general, property values increase over time. The longer you own a property, the more it appreciates in value. This appreciation is only possible when you buy and hold.

2. Sense Of Security

Owning a property that provides a stable, positive rental income is a very effective way to offset expenses and ensure continuous cash flow. For example, the most common lease agreements are for one year and are often automatically renewed. This provides investors with greater certainty and peace of mind about their earnings. In fact, the ability to have a steady cash flow every month is one of the most attractive features of buy-to-let real estate investment.

3. Not A Full-Time Job

Purchasing and maintenance are relatively inexpensive after the property is stabilized and leased. Most of the work required is done on the front end to acquire and lease the property. Unless you own a large amount of property, buying and maintaining it is usually not a full time job. This strategy is ideal for part-time investors, as it allows them to build a portfolio of rental properties on the side to supplement their income while continuing their day job.

4. The Headaches Of Being A Landlord

Having tenants is great, but it also means that you are dealing with independent adults who live on their own land. As a landlord, you have a legal obligation to maintain the property you are renting. Depending on what you buy, where you buy it, who you rent to, and sheer luck, the frequency of calls and complaints can vary greatly. However, there are a number of property management and people management issues that need to be dealt with on a regular basis. It can be incredibly stressful and irritating to be a landlord.

What strategy do you feel is best for you? Is it a fix and flip or a buy and hold? Regardless of your choice, keep the above tips in mind. Remember to research thoroughly and consider what you think you would like most simply. Both strategies are very profitable and a good investor can never go wrong with either. The question is not where to start, but when to start.

CHAPTER 2: The role of Cryptocurrencies, Smart Contracts, Daos and NFTs in the Metaverse

A Metaverse as we know now is a persistent online world where users can experience a richer immersive experience than existing online services through virtual and augmented reality interfaces.

However, like other applications of game-changing technologies, for example artificial intelligence (AI) and the Internet of Things (IoT), the Metaverse and blockchain are not concepts that evolve and exist in isolation. It is when they are applied together that their true potential is unlocked. This is because each of them has many features and functions that complement each other and can converge in a way that is more than the sum of its parts.

The important links between nfts, blockchains and the Metaverse

Virtual currencies

Let's start by looking at the most obvious use case for the blockchain in the Metaverse: money. Blockchains (decentralized databases protected by cryptography) are the basis of cryptocurrencies like Bitcoin, Litecoin, and Ether (the tokens of the Ethereum blockchain). The Metaverse promises to open up virtual worlds like Ready Player One, where we can play, work, and interact with our friends in immersive environments without ever leaving our homes. And, of course, anyone who understands human nature predicts that one of the most popular activities people will want to participate in while they are there is shopping and buying things!

It is already possible to use the cryptocurrency Mana to buy a plot of virtual real estate within Decentraland's online reality. In fact, it recently surfaced that someone did this and got up to $2.4 million. The government of Barbados recently joined the effort, using Decentraland to open the world's first Metaverse embassy.

But buying things will be just the beginning of blockchain-based money in the Metaverse. The rapidly growing field of decentralized finance (De-Fi) is perfectly suited to operate in a virtual world and environment, where Metaverse-based lending, trading and investing will become increasingly popular.

Gaming

Gaming is undoubtedly one of the most exciting use cases for the Metaverse, and here too, blockchain is driving innovation in this area. The Sandbox is a virtual world where anyone can create their own games and environments, and buy and sell digital goods and products using $Sand, an ethereum-based blockchain currency The Sandbox has already attracted several well-known brands, including Atari and Aardman, the creators of Shaun the Sheep The Sandbox is already home to well-known brands like Atari and Aardman Animations, the creators of Shaun the Sheep.

Crypto games are already big business, encompassing not only online casino games, but also the newer gaming paradigm that has come to be known as "Play-to-Earn." One of the most popular games at the moment is Axie Infinity, with over a million active users every day raising and fighting digital creatures that resemble Pokemon. Unlike Nintendo's game, however, winners are rewarded with cryptocurrency SLP, with top players earning around $250 per day. In developing countries, where this game is most popular, this represents a large income.

Another Metaverse game where players can earn cryptocurrencies that can be converted into real money is Oneto11, which bills itself as the world's first blockchain-based gaming ecosystem. Here, players can use their knowledge of the sport to compete with other players and earn the platform's own blockchain tokens (aka Oneto11).

If the Metaverse lives up to its hype, as everyone from Mark Zuckerberg to tech venture capitalists believe, blockchain gaming is expected to explode in the next few years.

NFTs

According to many predictions, NFTs (short for non-fungible tokens, Collins Dictionary's choice for the 2021 buzzword of the year) will play a major role in the Metaverse. NFTs are tokens that exist on the blockchain and can be used to prove ownership of connected digital assets. First of all, I've seen them used to trade digital artworks, but theoretically, they could be attached to anything:

virtual avatars, gaming assets, real estate (or should I say real estate?).

Accessing the realm of the Metaverse and proving that someone has the right to control who can visit or use a particular part of the virtual environment would be an important use (literally), he says. Many of the blockchain games that exist in the Metaverse also use NFTs as rewards (as an alternative to the other common type of blockchain token, cryptocurrency, which is generic and therefore not unique).

One of the main functions of NFTs in the Metaverse is to give value to objects. Since there are basically only 1s and 0s in the digital world, they can theoretically be reproduced and distributed indefinitely; NFTs can be used to prove that a person is the rightful owner of a particular object, thus providing a framework for assigning value to digital objects.

Decentralization

It's hard to say exactly how the Metaverse will work, because no one knows exactly how it will work yet. People like Mark Zuckerberg, of course, have their own ideas, and they invest a lot of money to make them happen. But will the reality be a centralized Metaverse controlled by corporations? Or will it be something more decentralized, like the blockchain concept? Blockchain, and its ability to enable smart contracts and decentralized autonomous organizations (DAOs), offers the potential for a different kind of digital realism, one that is not under the ownership of Silicon Valley megacorps. It can also be "owned" and governed by the people who use it, through participation in secure voting processes and the use of advanced blockchain features such as staking.

In fact, we could end up with something of each, with corporations building and maintaining their own metaphors for making rules, juxtaposed with the decentralized metaphor of public ownership: an avatar born and leveled in the public Metaverse run by the DAO, but now in the private Metaverse of Mark Zuckerberg. I wonder if avatars born and raised in the public Metaverse run by the DAO will be welcomed in the walled world of Mark Zuckerberg's private Metaverse. Who will have the final say in establishing basic social principles such as identity and property in the Metaverse? These are important questions, and there is no doubt that blockchain will play an important role in establishing the answers to them.

Key features of crypto Metaverses

Crypto Metaverses is still in the early stages of development, as are games that incorporate NFTs (non-perishable tokens). However, that doesn't mean that digital marketing can't be moved to the blockchain. In fact, experts predict that it could change the crypto world. In order to get the most out of Metaverse, users need to understand its key features.

Defining Features Of Metaverse In Cryptography

Metabarses have been around for a long time. The creators of the cryptoMetaverse distinguish the world from earlier versions by the following features

Decentralized

These worlds are decentralized because blockchain technology runs the cryptospace Metaverse. Blockchains can be configured in part or in full.

The cryptographic metaphor opens up a more unbiased form of interaction for users. Also, because it is decentralized, participants share ownership of it.

So it doesn't matter if the original creators of the Metaverse leave their world. The Metaverse will continue to exist.

Real world economic value

A crypto-Metaverse Cryptometabers rely on blockchain technology and cryptographic tokens. As such, their economy is tied to the larger economy in the crypto space.

Metaverse users can own a variety of items, including avatar skins, tokens, and virtual real estate. These items can be traded on the NFT market or on a decentralized exchange (DEX).

This means that Metaverse participants can demand real value for their Metaverse-based investments. Crypto-Metaverse users can exchange their items for goods in the same world or in another Metaverse. It is also possible to exchange items for investments that do not belong to the Metaverse.

Provenance

Goods in the crypto-Metaverse are usually provided in the form of tokens, such as NFTs. What these tokens represent varies from one virtual world to another.

If the Metaverse is a game where tasks are imposed on users, then a value can be assigned to various achievements or items. A good example of this is "Axie Infinity," one of the hottest crypto games of the moment.

When the Metaverse allows users to create, buy and sell virtual land, it can provide a way to monetize the experience. The Sandbox Metaverse is an outstanding example of this type of Metaverse in operation. NFTs help ensure the transparency of items in your game. It can also allow items to be linked to the asset market.

In addition, each NFT is unique. This makes it easy for users to code Metaverse items and tokens to verify the origin of content and assets in your game.

Governed By Users

In addition to owning the Metaverse, users have a degree of control over the virtual world in which they participate.

Some crypto-Metaverse give control to users through governance tokens. They also depend on

Decentralized Autonomous Organizations (DAOs). These channels allow participants to vote on changes and updates.

Metaverse games are a social and investment opportunity

As the Internet moves into its next phase of evolution, the Metaverse is moving ever closer to the forefront of what has been dubbed "Web 3.0."

According to crypto investment firm Grayscale, as the digital world continues to permeate our daily lives, the Metaverse has the potential to offer a market opportunity worth more than $1 trillion.

In a report published Thursday titled "Metaverse, Web 3.0, and the Virtual Cloud Economy," Grayscale's prediction is based on the opportunities created by the intersection of ongoing trends in our social lives and online gaming and the potential of blockchain to provide infrastructure for the digital world. It is based on the opportunities that arise.

In his statement, Grayscale stated that the market opportunity to enable the Metaverse is worth more than $1 trillion in yearly revenue and that it can compete with Web 2.0 businesses with a market value of $15 trillion today.

It is defined as "an interconnected, experiential, 3D virtual world where people interact in real time, wherever they are," according to the report's authors, David Grider and Matt Maximo. The Metaverse is "an Internet economy that spans the digital and physical world," according to Grider and Maximo. It is defined as follows.

It has the ability to revolutionize our social interactions, economic transactions, and the entire Internet economy," says the author of this future state of the web vision. They made a statement.

Grayscale believes that revenues from the virtual gaming world will grow from $180 billion in 2020 to at least $400 billion in 2025.

The shift in monetization by game developers is a key driver of the growth trend. The report points out that players are moving away from premium "pay to play" games to "free" games, with developers monetizing the sale of in-game items to players and allowing players to gain social status within the virtual world.

It also reports that crypto funding reached $8.2 billion in Q3 2021, of which $1.8 billion went to Web 3.0 and non-fungible tokens (NFTs).

Meanwhile, funding for gaming applications accounted for $1 billion, overshadowing all other NFT verticals in Q3.

The Metaverse is in "early entries"

Today, we spend about a third of our lives in leisure activities such as television, gaming and social media, and as remote working becomes the norm, Grayscale notes that this time will only get longer.

Particularly since the pandemic, much of our attention has been focused on digital activities, and the digital and physical worlds are slowly merging - This is also why the Metaverse is generating so much enthusiasm, and Facebook's recent renaming of itself as "Meta" is the most visible embrace of this increasingly new digital reality.

Seamless interoperability between the digital and the physical is also about owning digital items. Taking Decentraland, a leading blockchain-based project, as an example, a user logs in, plays the game, earns MANA, the native token of Decentraland, and the user can use it to buy NFTs or buy NFTs for the value of time spent in the game. We are creating an open-world Metaverse where users can use them to buy NFTs or create NFTs for the value of their time spent in the game.

Metaverse services will also expand beyond gaming. Earlier this month, Decentraland signed an agreement with the Caribbean nation of Barbados to legally declare digital real estate to build the world's first virtual embassy.

While open networks like Ethereum provide users with true ownership of digital items, the digital world before was a closed corporate metaphor owned by big tech companies that prohibited users from freely monetizing their investments and efforts.

Web 3.0's open crypto network solves this problem by "removing the capital controls imposed on these virtual worlds by Web 2.0 platforms," Grayscale argued.

Grayscale, which has witnessed a fresh wave of Metaverse investments, predicts that Web 2.0 technology businesses will soon recognize this inflection point and "will likely need to start exploiting the Metaverse to stay competitive."

In comparison to the $10 billion investment anticipated by corporations such as Facebook and the amount that could follow from other companies and venture capitalists, Metaverse virtual world users are reportedly'still in their infancy.' “However, if the growth rate maintains its current trajectory, this emerging segment has the potential to become dominant in the coming years.

Metaverse, Nft, DeFi: three crypto use cases that could redefine global priorities over time

Imagine attending a Taylor Swift concert in Los Angeles in the flesh, without having to book a ticket. But with Web 2.0 helping with connectivity, it's not enough to just watch the concert online. But in the Metaverse, you can experience the same thing without abandoning the real environment and without compromising the virtual atmosphere of the concert.

Also, from a crypto investment perspective, off-the-shelf tokens in the Metaverse, such as MANA and GALA, which serve as related trading entities in that virtual market, are getting a lot of attention. MANA's Decentraland, GALA's GALA Games, etc., if these meta-tokens grow As these meta-tokens grow, they may become even more popular.

NFT and the Age of New Ownership

Did you know that the NFT and the Metaverse are practically analogous these days? Confused?

NFT (Non-FungibleToken) is supposed to represent a whole new use case for crypto, but it has many similarities to the Metaverse.

There are many people's creative digital assets floating around in many Metaverse, such as galley games and dedicated gaming sandboxes. These assets and exclusives can then be traded as NFTs on the ecosystem, often using the currency associated with the Metaverse.

The gamification project by Metaverse has reinvented the wheel with respect to digital properties. People want to own and flaunt certain entities, and the best way to do so is to obtain the relevant NFTs.

NFTs also allow the creators of digital works, artwork, images, and other exclusive things to control their offerings. Since ownership is only verified through a blockchain ledger, it is transparent and can stop piracy and duplication.

In simple terms, NFTs are the link between the Metaverse and the real world, and providing them exclusively may benefit the real world.

Imagine that your favorite singer releases NFTs containing unedited parts of popular songs in the virtual space. Then, once 100 NFTs are sold, they launch a free meet and greet session every year to connect with the real world.

Also, given the relevance of the major crypto players, trading NFTs in the Metaverse may require trading native tokens.

Interestingly, the major crypto exchanges are actively listing Metaverse and NFT-related coins, and are fast tracking use cases.

Defi. Fintech Is Changing

Let's say you're in the Metaverse, or decent land, and suddenly you want to buy some virtual land. So you go to MANA. But how do you buy MANA in the first place, especially if you don't want to do it with fiat currencies, banks, or other intermediaries?

That's where DeFi Networks comes in, with its wide range of possibilities, including supporting native token trading between blockchains, smart contract-based lending and staking solutions, and P2P trading.

NFT, DAO, Mobileweb3 and the Metaverse: off and running in 2022

The year 2021 will go down in history as the year of NFT. It is also the year when Web3 awareness grows and visionaries, architects, developers and venture capitalists begin to imagine the next generation of public digital infrastructure: DAOs (decentralized autonomous organizations), dApps (decentralized applications) and cryptocurrencies are the next generation of Web3 Paving the decentralized way to the Metaverse: Facebook even rebranded itself as Meta.

As a new era of technology begins its evolutionary life cycle, the expectation of drama and controversy often manifests itself early on. The beginnings of 2022 have already shown how vibrant and frenetic Web3 can be. Bitcoin, Ethereum and altcoins gave up all of their big 2021 gains in January due to inflation fears and regulatory headwinds for crypto, while NFT stock exchange OpenSea announced a $13 billion valuation after a new funding round.

2022 is already up to the hype. New trends are shaping the Web3 business and the DAO is poised to become the cornerstone of the future of next generation digital infrastructure and blockchain technology.

New Kid In Town?

Over the course of more than a decade, the term "blockchain" has become synonymous with infrastructure and the cryptocurrency "Bitcoin," which is by many measurements the most popular cryptocurrency in the world Satoshi's brand genius should be recognized along with his mathematical and technical genius." Crypto" used to lead Google's search performance in the blockchain category; things began to change in early 2021 with the rise of NFTs, and by the end of the year NFTs had overtaken cryptos as the most used search term. This kind of crossover is an important trend to watch out for, as it is a great indicator of change.

Bitcoin is also under pressure from Ethereum as the developer's choice for building the foundation of Web3. Ethereum has the first-mover advantage of smart contracts and benefits from the "walled garden" approach that many developers have taken to building platforms in the Web 2.0 era.

DeFi and DAO models are gaining more ground through platforms that offer compatibility and interoperability with Ethereum. More than half of the top 20 ranked cryptocurrencies have an association with Ethereum through EVM compatibility or ERC-20 tokens, and tier 2 plays such as Polygon have become very popular by 2021.

NFTs are beginning to change the demographics of crypto consumers, with more and more women, especially millennials, turning to the medium as a renaissance and profit center for art and collecting. according to Statisa, women are competing with men, accounting for nearly half of NFT owners across all age groups. They represent almost half of all NFT owners in all age groups. Compared to cryptocurrencies, where 90% of Bitcoin users are men, this is a significant demographic shift, and one that product marketers are not ignoring.

NFT represents a big step in the right direction to increase social diversity in crypto and digital goods; women like Hackatao and Grimes lead the way; FEWOCiOUS is a transgender, physically untouchable teenager who famously disrupted Christie's online auction system. The arts, sports and entertainment business is driven by young people and multicultural communities, but anyone can start in this field and NFT opens more doors.

Nft Removes Barriers

Traditional distribution channels, from grocery stores to linear television, better understand that they can be catalysts for connecting the masses to NFT. Mobile operators, for example, are paving the way by delivering NFT directly from their decks. Telcos around the world have the advantage of having their platform in the hands of almost every human being on the planet, and companies are looking to this advantage for their next generation exchanges.

GFTX, a nascent NFT exchange based on the West Coast, along with True Mobile, a leading telecom company serving over 60 million subscribers, has launched a "load to phone number" model in Thailand. New subscribers can unlock the NFT and journey into the world of digital assets and Metaverse communities with a simple login using their phone number. Most notably, subscribers do not need to understand the intricacies of blockchain and cryptography. Charging for numbers is frictionless, easy to use, and has zero barriers to entry.

The ability to offer NFT or enable NFT transactions should not be rocket science," said Jonas Hudson, co-founder of GFTX. Currently, users have to go through 10 or more steps in any number of markets to get NFTs; it's not Web 3, it's Web 2.0. The average consumer is not willing to provide personal information, even for services they know and need. In order to make each consumer's journey simple, fast and exciting, it is essential to grease the wheels. GFTX makes the end-to-end creation and transaction of NFTs as easy as purchasing a cell phone call, which many consumers are familiar with. In other words, GFTX has made it easy for the masses. In short, GFTX is the mobile NFT marketplace for the masses."

Carriers also have the advantage of being able to engage with their subscribers more easily than many other distribution channels. By offering NFTs that can provide consumers with coupons, discounts and special offers, telcos can open up relationships with other consumer sectors and create a platform to offer new products and special offers to new and existing customers.

The true potential of NFT is yet to be imagined. It is a smart currency that self-manages and settles transactions between buyers and sellers, without the artwork today and the expensive and opaque middlemen tomorrow. Visible and personal to consumers and business users, the mobile wallet is a secure and dynamic transaction platform that accepts, creates, stores, and transacts value, connecting marketers directly with mainstream consumers. This phenomenon has been applied to almost every industry, including the fast-growing mobile coupon and loyalty services. Brands, large and small, have never before been able to speak to consumers on a one-on-one basis in specific and relevant terms. This is made possible by Mitch Chait, co-founder of GFTX.

Intellectual property in Web 3

NFTs and DAOs upend the traditional IP model: in 2017, Cryptokitties created a revolutionary model for IP rights, giving NFT rights holders the ability to earn revenue from their IP. This is essentially a license agreement wrapped in code.

This, of course, leads to the question of "who owns the underlying data?

CryptoKitties was one of the first NFT licenses to allow the transfer and use of artwork associated with user-owned "kitty" works. What was most interesting was that it included commercial rights up to $100,000 per year. This is where the BAYC (Bored Ape Yacht Club) was inspired to create a model similar to "Kitties".

This is a counter-Disney model, where a centralized company owns all the IP verticals and licenses, and distributes them to other companies and individuals who focus on their core business. For example, BAYC doesn't brew beer, so they let the owners of "Monkey" use their brand to create products. For young artists and companies that don't have the means to vertically accelerate their business, this brings new product extensions and new revenue. The next big brands may be decentralized and owned by the "masses," Hudson says.

There are issues of rights beyond art and entertainment, and addressing ownership issues regarding medical records, legal documents, and other IP moved from wallet to wallet. the NFT and DAO can manage the rule sets, but politicians and legislators will have to make sure that identity and personal (sensitive) data is as identity and personal (sensitive) data moves from wallet to wallet, we will likely be discussing many of these issues for some time.

Is NFT a security?

In 2022, all roads lead to the SEC. the 2017 ICO fiasco caused a lot of grief for unsuspecting investors who plunked their money into tokens that promised 100x+ returns.The SEC was quick to quash what it saw as the "Wild West" of unsecured token offerings, and the same looks set to happen in 2022 with some DeFi and NFT products that look more like securities than collectibles.

In London, the Tube (public tube/subway) is full of ads promoting NFTs and crypto, and the UK advertising regulator has cracked down, hitting Papa John's with a recall notice for offering BTC on demand.

What will change in 2022 is the transition from an open NFT platform to an SEC-regulated NFT platform.

"Past" and "future" are converging in the "present". the exponential power and adaptability of NFTs and their global scalability through seamless interfaces will have to come to terms with the regulatory regime in the near future. AML, KYC and investor protection through "code is law" and DeFi. The power of NFTs and how they are used will be evaluated both as rewards and collectibles, which are clearly not securities, and as NFTs, where ownership is fractionalized and valuations and rates of return are provided. The power of NFTs and how they are used will be evaluated in two ways: as rewards or as collectibles that are clearly not securities, and as NFTs that fractionalize ownership and provide a valuation or rate of return.

The latter could turn an NFT into a cash instrument by creating an investment contract, i.e. a security or other financial instrument. As regulators, policymakers and legislators seek to understand and, in some cases, control DeFi and NFTs, we will see increased regulatory oversight and enforcement of NFTs globally, and continue our march forward.

New regulations will allow physical ownership of NFTs and NFTs will allow private investors to own a portion of Picasso and DAO shares. This change in asset ownership eliminates the 'insider' advantage and provides a level playing field for investors. Vince Molinari, founder of Fintech.tv, says, "Along with mobile and social media, everyone can legally use these new investment instruments. It is now possible for everyone to legally use these new investment instruments," says Vince Molinari, founder of Fintech.tv.

Long the "hype" of the Metaverse

In short, in reality, the rush to "Metaverse", especially in the young decentralized economy, will make massive inroads in 2022. Right now, the NFT space is struggling. The lower scale markets are doing minimal business, even with 20 million monthly users, and the less distributed markets are generating $200,000 per month in revenue, much of it based on one or two NFT releases driving the numbers.

OpenSea has lost half its business since August, most wash marketers are looking the other way, and this trend will likely continue. In short, there are no new customers and many early stage NFTs have peaked in the crypto community.

The next big thing everyone is clinging to is the Metaverse, and the players who are winning are the players clinging to their walled gardens. The distributed Metaverse has very few users, and the reason for that is that the polygon count is not enough for the main players/players/masses.

If you ask players to jump into your Metaverse and the shrinkage factor is terrible, they will quickly flee. The Metaverse has to be mobile first, and the technology is too fast. You can have avatars, you can wear clothes, you can go to clubs, you can dance. But if the Metaverse doesn't have the mobile-friendly features to reach the mainstream, it probably won't get far.

Game companies are still hesitant to open up their walled gardens and embrace decentralized assets on a large scale. This will likely change in the medium to long term. Commercials with models looking at trips to life in museum paintings aren't ready yet, and users will still have to use VR head pieces connected to a $4,500 computer to actually make them work.

It's not meta, and user-friendly, low polygon-count games like Fortnite and Roblox will continue to lead the way here. Marketplaces will also have to be able to trade assets on the blockchain at the same speed as current trade rails to compete.

As we enter 2022 and begin building the Metaverse, what is clear is that NFT has dramatically changed the landscape of participation in the crypto ecosystem in just over a year. The space has expanded beyond the male-dominated Bitcoin tribe to include users from more diverse and balanced walks of life, giving them easier access to an ecosystem that provides valuable social and commercial utility.

The growing number of more traditional product companies and distribution channels that see an opportunity to better engage customers in the form of art, collectibles, swag, coupons, rewards, and financial products has also broadened the social base for accepting crypto. The emergence of many new NFT products and investments is imminent, and DAO-enabled networks have the power to supersize these products.

The move to a simple NFT wallet tied to a cell phone number is another step in reducing the friction for consumers to access highly practical crypto products and services without a technical understanding of how the crypto engine works. We are getting to the point where we can just push the ON BUTTON button and walk away.

All of these factors are sound early indicators that the NFT is a bridgehead for building the Metaverse and will help us better deliver on the promise of inclusion through mass social and business adoption of crypto products and digital goods in the emerging world of Web3.

A look-in on DAOs

This past summer, a group of "crypto-fans" pooled their money and invested a seven-figure sum in a... They secretly purchased Wu-Tang Clan's only surviving album, Once Upon a Time in Shaolin, for a total of $4 million.

However, it was not until Wednesday that an organization called PleasrDAO came forward as a buyer. The announcement came as a pleasant surprise to the crypto community and made headlines in major media outlets.

PleasrDAO is no newcomer to the world of rare collectibles, and already had a portfolio full of multi-million dollar assets; in June, it purchased the original "Doge" meme non-fungible token (NFT) for $4 million.

But what makes the PleasrDAO acquisition stand out is that while it may sound like a typical investment firm, it is not. As the name suggests, it is a decentralized autonomous organization (DAO) and is powered by blockchain technology.

Recently, some DAOs have begun to attract the interest of more mainstream investors, with billionaire Mark Cuban calling them "the ultimate combination of capitalism and progressivism. Venture capitalist Andriessen Horowitz (a16z) has also led multi-million dollar funding rounds for both individual DAOs and the companies that helped create them.

Members of the crypto community predict that DAOs will be the "next big trend" in the space, and as mainstream investors begin to take notice, you may be wondering, what exactly is a DAO?

Here's what you need to know, from how it works to what experts think may compete with traditional business structures in the near future.

Internet communities that share bank accounts".

DAOs come in all shapes and structures, but simply put, "a DAO is an Internet community that shares a bank account," Cooper Turley, who has built several popular DAOs with investors, told CNBC Make It.

Basically, it's a small group of people coming together to form a chat group and raise money using an ethereum wallet," Turley said. From there, they will decide how to raise the funds needed for the DAO's mission.

Many DAOs fall into two broad categories: those that co-manage open source or blockchain-based projects, and those that make investments. They can act like a limited liability company (LLC), a venture capital firm, or an investment firm like PleasrDAO.

The specifics of the type, structure, rules, and governance of a DAO will depend on the group and its purpose.

For those who witnessed the first DAO hack in 2016, when millions of dollars were effectively stolen, the term can have a negative connotation. While still a risk, DAO has made great strides since then.

Types of DAOs

It's important to understand that DAO is a broad term that encompasses many different types of groups and businesses; even though the two collectives are quite different, they are both still DAOs.

Here is an example of a well-known DAO:

- PleasrDAO collects a variety of NFTs and invests them in other assets.

- Black women and non-binary artists are encouraged to submit ideas to HerStory DAO, which aggregates and funds them
- Komorebi Collective DAO funds women and non-binary crypto founders.
- Friends with Benefits DAO is an exclusive social club that you pay to join.
- MetaCartel Venture DAO is a for-profit business that invests in early-stage decentralized apps.

How a DAO works

To comprehend DAOs, it is necessary to first comprehend the technology that underpins them.Most DAOs rely on blockchain technology and smart contracts (a collection of codes that works on a blockchain).

A blockchain is a decentralized digital ledger. It is commonly known for publicly documenting transactions in various cryptocurrencies like Bitcoin and other digital assets like NFT, but the blockchain can be used in many other ways. in the case of the DAO, the blockchain acts as the backbone, maintaining every structure and rules can be maintained on a chain.

In a traditional organization, there is usually a hierarchy. A formal board of directors, executives and top management have the power to decide on structure and make changes.

DAOs, on the other hand, are decentralized, meaning that they are not governed by one person or organization. The rules and governance of each DAO are codified in smart contracts on the blockchain and cannot be changed without a vote of the DAO members.

Instead of a few people having the majority of the say, the members of each DAO can generally vote together on decisions on an equal footing.

For example, PleasrDAO members collectively decided to buy a Wu-Tang Clan album. PleasrDAO members are co-owners of the NFT deed and share ownership of the album.

Sometimes in larger DAOs, a team is formed around a leader with voting rights to work on different aspects of the organization. This way, all members do not have to vote on every nuance.

The most important aspect of a DAO, says Turley, is transparency: all decisions within the DAO are made, debated, voted on, and documented publicly.

DAOs structure

The structure of every DAO is different, but generally when you join a DAO, you agree to its code. Changing that code is not easy, and changes usually require a vote among the members.

The DAO is "very participatory," says Aaron Wright, co-founder and CEO of OpenLaw, a blockchain-based protocol for creating and enforcing legal contracts. Mr. Wright has aided in the development of various decentralized autonomous organizations (DAOs), notably FlamingoDAO, which collects NFTs.

"In order to make a decision, you do not have to wait until there is a quorum or enough individuals to vote," says the author.It operates by consensus, just like the Internet," Wright explains. If enough people support a project, that project is decided.

To gain voting rights or membership in a DAO, one typically purchases governance tokens, which are cryptocurrencies tied to a particular project; for some DAOs, governance tokens are only available in structured funding rounds, and sometimes demand exceeds the amount of tokens available. By owning these tokens, members typically own shares in the DAO and can help shape the future of the DAO.

Although it varies from DAO to DAO, the weight of a member's vote usually depends on the amount they have contributed to the project.

If a DAO does not use a governance token, Wright explains, it can accept other forms of investment, such as Ether, the second largest cryptocurrency by market value, because the Ethereum blockchain powers most DAOs. However, each DAO still has its own system.

In addition to voting rights, members can also work for that DAO. It is common to have several internal positions, including those for token distribution and financial management.

Working for ownership means working for the tokens," says Turley. For example, he is paid mainly in governance tokens for his work in the DAO, but he may also be paid in ETH or USDC.

Challenges and unknowns

Despite their growing popularity, DAOs have a long way to go before they are fully integrated.

"Not all DAOs will work. In fact, the majority of DAOs will not be successful in the long run.They are very ephemeral in nature," says Turley. It's a very dangerous area to poke around in."

There is always the possibility that the value of a DAO's tokens could fall to zero. Potential investors should do their homework first and spend only the amount they can afford to lose.

However, there are also significant potential advantages, says Mr. Turley. For example, governor tokens often have a secondary market value. Owning a governor token is like owning a stake in an early stage start-up, and if successful later, the stake can be very valuable.

DAOs will also need to overcome a number of potential regulatory and legal challenges, particularly in the US. There are a number of unknowns about how the potential legal structure in the US will affect the DAO and how it operates.

The problem in all areas right now is the lack of clarity in regulation," says Luis Ramalho, co-founder of Polvo Technologies, a company that develops machine learning strategies for trading Bitcoin and digital assets. Ramalho was also involved in the creation of FingerprintsDAO, which collects NFTs.

Looking To The Future

Although there are unknowns, those involved believe that DAOs will have a disruptive impact on traditional business structures.

I think the DAO is the new LLC," Turley said. I think in five years, there will be no equity in companies. They will have tokens and be represented as DAOs."

Billionaire investor Mark Cuban also sees value in DAOs, he says." He tweeted in May, "The future of the enterprise could change dramatically as DAOs take over legacy businesses." Entrepreneurs who make DAOs happen will make money." When a community has good governance, everyone benefits.

Cuban acknowledges that DAOs are "not suitable for all types of companies," but believes that "there are so many functions and processes that can make any company more efficient and productive if they use a decentralized and reliable approach."

The recent spate of institutional investment in DAOs is another sign of growth for the industry. It also indicates the potential for more widespread adoption and the possibility of competing with traditional companies and organizations.

Turley predicts that the mega-popular and successful companies of the future could be DAOs." I think the next Facebook-type company will be founded as a DAO, not an LLC.

Explaining web 3.0: from the Blockchain and crypto to Nft and Metaverse

Last week, Jack Dorsey took to Twitter to slam the hot-button tech trend known as Web3, cautioning consumers and dismissing it as a tool for venture capitalists to promote cryptocurrencies... and author Tim O'Reilly, who coined the term Web 2.0 in 2004. Tim O'Reilly, the author who coined the term Web 2.0 in 2004, warned this month that it was premature to get excited about Web 3. Time magazine's Person of the Year, Elon Musk, dismisses it simply: "Web3 is like bs.

Really? Web3 is the hottest buzzword in the tech world. But the term is indefinite and rapidly evolving, and its meaning often changes depending on who is talking about it.

Web3 is a term used by enthusiasts to describe the next phase of the Internet, featuring Internet services and mobile applications reimagined on top of decentralized blockchain technology. It often covers a wide range of emerging technologies such as cryptocurrencies, DAOs, NFTs (non-fungible tokens) and other digital assets. There are also enthusiasts who associate games, Metaverse, augmented reality and virtual reality with Web3.

This is due to the fact that some virtual worlds rely on blockchain-based digital assets.

Chris Dixon, general partner of venture capital firm Andreessen Horowitz, said in an article published on the firm's website that Web3 is a builder and user-owned Internet, organized by tokens.

Web3 supporters like Dixon say that building with blockchain technology will force companies to be interoperable and "give users ownership: the ability to own a piece of the Internet." Skeptics, however, argue that it is dishonest to advocate for decentralized technology from the user's perspective, since VCs are heavily invested in the underlying mechanisms of Bitcoin and Web3. Dorsey said that Web3 "finally has a centralized entity with a different label.

Okay, so what does that mean? CBS News asked technology experts for a basic description of Web3 and why it is or is not important.

What's Driving The Hype?

Facebook's rebranding as Meta in October and the tech giant's new support for cryptocurrency likely brought Web3's ideas about blockchain and decentralized technology into the mainstream,

"Techmeme Ride Home" podcast host Brian McCullough, host of the Techmeme Ride Home podcast, said.

Web3 is a repackaging of certain technologies," McCullough told CBS News. Blockchain has fallen into a kind of dead-end tech culture, and consumers are sick of the hype. Traditional crypto will never become a mainstream currency, NFT has become a cult, VR has been the 'next big thing' for decades, and Web3 is a brand that plausibly brings these ideas together."

According to McCullough, Web3 is hot right now because Silicon Valley influencers like Dorsey and Musk, and venture capitalists like Andriessen Horowitz, started talking about it after Facebook's pivot." He said, "The technology is not new, but the marketing is new. Built for business, "not for consumers.

TechRepublic editor-in-chief Bill Detwiler says it's time to ignore the Web3 hype and focus on the business technology: the core blockchain technology behind Web3 is "real, powerful, and built for the enterprise, not the consumer."

In the current technology paradigm, Detweiler points out, the cloud is thought of as the data storage, computing power, and SaaS offerings of companies like Amazon, Google, Microsoft, and Oracle. Ethereum founder and Web3 pioneer Gavin Wood envisions a new economy built around the blockchain, where individuals can provide direct services to each other, no company owns or controls the system, and the ability to trade things of value is inherent in the system. But the revolutionary decentralization of the system is not yet complete.

But revolutionary decentralization? That's still a long way off, Detweiler says.

The wood vision requires a major social, political and economic transformation," he says. Companies are currently using blockchain to track lettuce from the farm to the supermarket," Detwiler explains. It's not revolutionary, but it's realistic.

Marcus Estes, founder of cannabis distribution company Chroma Signet, also agrees that Web3 technology is built for business, not consumers." We are using the public blockchain to help small cannabis companies launch limited edition products in certain areas of Detroit," he explained. 'We are providing an unlicensed solution that is applied by the blockchain, not by people, so we couldn't do that with previous web technologies. It's an evolution of the open source business model."

The Bottom Line

The enthusiasm and attacks on Web3 may be motivated by personal motives for Musk, Dorsey, and other big-tech founders, according to Drew Olanoff, a startup analyst and former TechCrunch Venture Capital reporter. It's fun to watch them argue on Twitter, but I don't take it seriously."

"I collect sports jerseys, and I understand the appeal of collectors like NFT," says Olanoff. It may be revolutionary in the future, but I don't think it will be, Web3 is just a marketing term, just like Web 2.0."

Podcaster McCullough agrees. A new form of cryptocurrency could indeed be the currency of the Metaverse, he points out. NFTs and digital items could become our clothes, our identity, our status sign. And VR could become more than just a sidebar to games. That's cool, but it's not real," he explained. "For now, Web3 technology is still primitive; it's plausible that blockchain technology, along with AR and VR, could be the next big thing, but not today."

CHAPTER 3: Virtual Reality

Meaning of Virtual Reality (VR)?

Virtual reality is a technology that allows people to feel as if they are immersed in a physical environment while performing actions in a digital environment. The artificial environment is experienced through sensory stimuli provided by a computer, and your actions can influence what happens in the digital environment.

The goal of VR is to allow people to experience and manipulate their environment as if it were the real world. In its current stage of development, users need to interact with this kind of artificial environment by wearing a headset or gloves for position tracking.

Virtual reality should not be confused with simple 3D environments, such as those found in computer games. Rather than being personally part of a virtual world, virtual reality allows the user to experience and manipulate the environment through an avatar. The best virtual reality allows the user to be fully immersed.

There are no specific standards for the virtual reality experience, so opinions differ depending on the industry and the mode of virtual reality that is used to achieve it. However, there are some general guidelines that can be applied to virtual reality.

The image should consist of a life-size view of the user or viewer (unless the expected effect is different from this).

The system performing virtual reality must be able to track the user's movements, in particular eye and head movements, to change the image on the display or to initiate relevant events.

Basic terms and concepts

Immersion

Immersion is the act of placing the user in an artificial environment and making them feel like they are there; VR creates this immersive playground, where sights, sounds, and perceived emotions surround the user and make them feel like they are there.

Interactivity

When we talk about virtual reality, interactivity refers to the special relationship that is established between a digital model and its user. It refers to the user's ability to participate in the transmission process, and to the user's ability to participate in the process.Therefore, a medium is interactive if the user has the possibility to influence the content and form of the communication. There are levels of interaction: at the lowest level, the user simply selects information; at the middle level, the user can create or insert content; and at the highest level, the virtual environment responds appropriately to the user's input. Immersiveness in virtual reality should only be properly understood in immersive simulations, where the user interacts with the environment through all five senses. However, it usually refers to spatial simulations that are available only through vision, i.e., screens that give the impression that the user can move freely.

Sensory feedback

Although virtual reality (VR) provides a multimodal channel for sensory feedback, it is highly dependent on visual information.... This suggests that additional feedback from visual modalities is suboptimal and that using a fully multimodal interface will be more effective.

Degrees of freedom

When talking about motion and tracking in VR, it is often referred to as "degrees of freedom" or "DoF". More degrees of freedom mean that more body movements can be tracked by the headset and mapped to the simulated representation.

If you read books about degrees of freedom, you will often come across the two terms 3DoF and 6DoF (three and six degrees of freedom, respectively). Headsets that offer only 3DoF only track head movements (roll, tilt, yaw), but not position in space (x, y, z coordinates). 6DoF is able to track both head movements and coordinates in physical space.

Today, most VR headsets offer full position tracking with 6DoF, and many older mobile headsets and standalone headsets that are being discontinued or phased out, such as Google Cardboard, Google Daydream, Gear VR, and Oculus Go, offer 3DoF. Many older mobile headsets and standalone headsets that are being discontinued or phased out, such as Google Cardboard, Google Daydream, Gear VR, and Oculus Go, use 3DoF.

Field of view

FOV is an abbreviation for Field of View, which translates to "viewing angle" in Japanese. In terms of our eyes, the field of view refers to everything that we can see at any given moment.

In the case of a VR headset, the Field of View refers to everything you can see at any given time in the virtual world when you are using the headset. Currently available VR headsets have a field of view that is smaller than what the eye can see, that is, the VR environment does not fill the eye's field of view.

As a result, when you use VR, you often get a black "rim" around the lens you are looking through. This is, simply put, the space around the lens inside the headset. However, if the headset's field of view is wide enough, the border can give the impression that you are looking at the virtual world through glasses, making you forget that there is a border. There are different ways to measure the field of view, and device manufacturers may not specify exactly how much you can see compared to other headsets.

Controllers

In the VR environment, there are many forms of content that can be interactively simulated. In order to control these simulations, some kind of controller is required.

Some high-end headsets, such as the HTC Vive Cosmos, Oculus Quest, and Oculus Rift S, come with two-handed controllers.

PlayStation also offers VR. Some games require the brand's Move controllers, but it is also possible to use the regular PS4™ DualShock controllers.

Other products include the Valve Index, a controller that wraps around the palm of your hand or finger joint and detects finger movement and pressure. This controller is unlike any other controller currently on the market.

Facebook's Oculus Quest has hand-tracking technology, which eliminates the need for a controller. The headset can detect the length of your hand and finger movements with much higher accuracy.

Tracking

Tracking is very important for a complete VR experience. Tracking is the process of telling the computer where you are looking and what you are doing so that it can accurately render the virtual world around you. The more accurate your tracking, the more comfortable your VR experience will be.

Virtual rooms

A VR room is a self-contained area equipped with embedded and wearable technology to provide or enhance a multimedia virtual reality experience. Unlike seated or stationary VR, VR rooms allow you to move around freely, creating a more lifelike experience VR rooms are often used for virtual reality games.

The Virtual Reality Room was the first choice for the realization of a virtual environment.

VR session duration

Recent data shows that the average session duration for virtual reality (VR) users in the US was 19.7 minutes in the second and third quarters of 2019. First-time users had an average session duration of 16.1 minutes, while repeat users had an average session duration of 20.4 minutes.

V.R. head-mounted visor: A set of glasses or helmet with a small monitor in front of each eye that produces a three-dimensional image that the wearer sees

Types of virtual reality

Augmented Reality

Augmented reality is a type of virtual reality that allows the user to see the real world, usually through a cell phone screen, and make virtual changes on the screen. A good example to help you better understand augmented reality is the mobile gaming app Pokémon Go. You can activate your phone's camera and point it at a location where you think Pokémon might be. Your phone's screen will then show the Pokémon as if they were in the picture frame. It only appears in the screen environment, there is no physical addition to the location where the photo is taken.

Collaborative VR

A type of virtual reality that allows users in different locations to come together in a virtual environment in the form of a 3D projected character. 3D virtual characters from different players come together in the virtual environment of a mobile game such as PlayerUnknowns Battlegrounds (PUBG). PlayersUnknowns Battlegrounds (PUBG) is a good example of Collaborative VR, as it brings together 3D virtual characters from different players, all interacting as virtual people in a virtual environment.

Impervious VR

Impervious Virtual Reality is a type of Virtual Reality where you interact with a virtual environment, usually through a computer, and can control some characters and activities within it, The virtual environment, on the other hand, does not directly interact with the user

A good example of non-penetrative virtual reality is a computer game like Dota 2. You can control your own character, which in turn influences the virtual environment of the game. Technically, you are interacting with the virtual environment, but not directly. It is your character in the game that does this.

Non-immersive VR

Non-immersive VR is a form of reality where users are provided with a computer-generated surroundings without having the usual feel of being immersed in the digital world. The most important nature of a non-immersive digital world system lies in the fact that users are fully aware of happenings taking place around them.

This system makes use of computer input devices e.g mouse, keyboard etc or video game consoles to manipulate the digital content being displayed.

Fully immersive VR

Fully immersive virtual reality is the opposite of non-immersive virtual reality. It guarantees a realistic virtual experience. You will feel as if you are physically present in the virtual world and that the events that are taking place there are happening to you.

In order to provide a realistic virtual experience, special equipment is required, such as VR goggles, gloves, and body detectors with sensory detectors. Data from these sensors is used by the computer and the virtual world reacts to it in real time to provide the user with a realistic virtual experience.

For example, in a virtual game zone, you and other players can simultaneously interact with the virtual environment and play against each other using special equipment.

Semi-immersive VR

Semi-immersive virtual reality is an intermediate virtual reality between non-immersive virtual reality and fully immersive virtual reality. It allows you to move around in a virtual environment using a computer screen or VR glasses, but other than the visual experience, there are no physical sensations to enhance the experience.

Virtual tours are a good example of semi-subconscious virtual technology. They can be device-based or web-based. Many companies are adopting this technology because it allows participants to walk through a location without actually being there.

Major players

Facebook/Oculus

In 2014, Facebook acquired Oculus, a VR company focused on creating VR headsets and software for developers. Oculus developed the popular Oculus Rift and oculus Go headsets, as well as the first all-in-one VR gaming system, the next Oculus was one of the first VR companies to gain significant public traction, and has since worked to streamline the headset while creating games, educational and entertainment software for the device. While their main goal is to create products focused on the gaming industry, they are also working in areas such as 3D video and photography, and are rumored to be working on an ARdevice.

HTC and Valve

The HTC Vive is a virtual reality system created jointly by Valve (developer of the Steam digital game store) and HTC (manufacturer of high-end consumer electronics). It offers a standard Vive headset and an enhanced Vive Pro. Each is relatively affordable compared to competing products and is primarily focused on the entertainment and gaming industries.

Both headsets support motion tracking with the highly accurate Beacon tracking system, making them one of the best room-scale VR experiences available. HTC and Valve will continue to work together with the goal of bringing VR to the mainstream as quickly as possible and continuing to create high-quality, yet affordable products.

Alphabet/Google

Daydream is a portable virtual reality headset that is compatible with a wide range of mobile devices. In addition to allowing developers to create immersive VR experiences through YouTube videos and mobile apps, the VR headset has been used to create "The Female Planet," an empathetic look at women's leadership, an augmented reality CPR trainer, and an immersive Ocean to Plate," a documentary on the fishing supply chain, and many other humanities and education projects.

Cardboard is Google's virtual reality headset, and as we all know, it's made of cardboard. By making the product simple and affordable, Google has been able to gain a large number of VR individuals. In addition to providing consumers with an affordable VR headset, they are using it to promote initiatives such as Google Expeditions (a way for students to go on field trips without leaving the classroom) and Google Jump (a camera made for 3D recording).

Microsoft

HoloLens is an enterprise mixed reality project from Microsoft. While a typical AR/VR headset requires a connection to a computer and a controller, HoloLens is an all-in-one product, so users only need a headset. it runs on Windows 10 and uses the Mixed Reality features built into the OS. The unit currently costs $5,000 due to its high tech density, so for now Microsoft is offering it to businesses on a rental basis until it becomes more affordable.

iTechArt

iTechArt specializes in custom development of Augmented Reality (AR) and Virtual Reality (VR) software. iTechArt provides users with the tools to make VR and AR as iTechArt provides users with tools that allow them to utilize VR and AR as they wish.

iTechArt does more than just provide tools so that users can do what they want with VR. iTechArt is also known for its customer service. This is a company that teaches users how to get the most out of their services.

This is accomplished with virtual reality software that teaches them how to play, experience, and create with the company's VR programs. In addition, iTechArt supports 360-degree video, which allows users to use a variety of devices and is cross-platform.

Samsung

Samsung is able to provide users with an incredible experience in an immersive virtual environment thanks to its Gear VR lenses.

"The creation of these Samsung virtual reality products aims to open up new ways of communicating with users and helping people in different fields through innovative experiences", said Terry Weech, IM Sales Manager for Samsung Latin America.

Samsung presents the new Galaxy S8 and S8+ accompanied by a more optimized VR Gear with a remote control to better handle the motion sensor between the hand and the lens, and it is also careful in the content it offers to its users: BuzzFeed and NowThis. Users can choose content from a wide catalog of apps, including interactive 360-degree news, movies, concerts and sports games.

Unity

Given their reputation for producing games with high quality graphics, it's no surprise that they're getting into the VR business. Like other virtual reality companies, Unity offers users the opportunity to create high quality, immersive VR programs.

Unity not only enables such creations, but also encourages them by providing creators with Unity Learn. Unity Learn offers live sessions and over 750 hours of videos to help creators hone their skills.

You can also submit your work and Unity will check its potential.

VR outside gaming application

Apart from gaming, there are so many uses and application of the virtual reality. They are listed below;

Education

In 2015, Google launched the Expeditions Pioneer program, which includes Asus smartphones, Expedition features tablets for teachers to run field trips, routers that can operate without an Internet connection, and a library of over 100 virtual trips that can take students anywhere from the Eiffel Tower to the Great Wall of China.

New platforms such as LectureVR and AltspaceVR also hope to bring new educational possibilities to educators everywhere, providing the technology to create avatars and conduct "multiplayer" sessions with unparalleled interaction and social interaction. Toyota is already using the Oculus headset as part of its TeenDrive365 campaign, designed to educate teens and parents about the dangers of distracted driving. The company believes that the immersive experience offered by VR headsets has the potential to revolutionize education across the board.

Social Applications

VR is currently being used for applications other than gaming, such as real estate, manufacturing, design, quality control, architecture, training and education. But the potential is much greater. Certainly, consumer applications such as storytelling, security and IoT systems have the potential to become a very large market in the future. And many of the uses of software originally designed for games can be adapted and modified for other purposes.

Healthcare

Healthcare has been an early adopter of Virtual Reality. In the past, it has been used for skills training, surgical simulation, robotic surgery and phobia treatment. V.R allows healthcare professionals to practice new skills or update existing ones in a safe environment without putting the patient at risk. Virtual reality simulations, such as Surgical Theater and Conquer Mobile, can use real diagnostic images, such as CAT scans and ultrasound, to create highly detailed 3D models of a patient's anatomy.

Surgeons can use this virtual model to locate tumors, make surgical incisions, and determine the safest and most efficient way to perform complex operations. In addition, virtual reality can also be an attractive and effective rehabilitation tool. In Europe, a company called MindMaze is using immersive virtual reality therapy to help patients suffering from brain damage. This therapy can help restore motor and cognitive function faster than traditional physical therapy. According to the company, MindMaze's virtual exercises and real-time feedback are designed to feel like a game and help motivate patients to practice the activities they need in their daily lives.

Fashion

Although not well known, VR is also being used in the fashion field and is having a significant impact. For example, virtual simulations of store environments are very useful for retailers to design signage and product displays without having to completely build them as they would in the real world. Similarly, adequate time and resources can be allocated to building store layouts. Some of the popular brands that have already started implementing VR into their businesses include: Tommy Hilfiger, Coach, and Gap. These brands are using VR to provide a 360-degree experience of fashion shows and allow customers to try on items virtually.

CHAPTER 4: Augmented Reality

There are several different types of augmented reality in use today. From marketing to gaming, many companies are in the process of exploring the use of this new technology. The question is, how do you make use of it? That's easier asked than answered.

To better understand how AR can be used, let's take a look at the different types and some examples of each.

Types of Augmented Reality

Marker-based augmented reality

Marker-based AR is a type of augmented reality that uses markers to initiate an augmented experience. Markers are often made up of QR codes or other unique designs that act as anchors for the technology. When a marker in the physical world is recognized by an augmented reality application, digital content is placed on top of it.

Marker-based augmented reality is typically used for marketing and retail purposes. Imagine a talking business card or a moving brochure.

In this example, marker-based AR is being used for retail in someone's home. Imagine if you could see what a new bathroom vanity would look like before you actually bought it. In addition, the app allows you to step through the different sink options to see which one is best suited for the space.

Markerless AR

Markerless AR is more versatile than marker AR because it allows the user to decide where to place the virtual object. It's a completely digital way to experience. It allows you to experience different styles and locations completely digitally, without moving from your environment at all.

Markerless AR relies on the hardware of the device, such as the camera, GPS, digital compass, accelerometer, etc., to collect the information needed for the AR software to do its job.

In this example, the virtual car can be placed anywhere, regardless of its surroundings. The Mustang itself can be customized, the display can be adjusted and rotated, and additional information about the product can be learned.

The following augmented realities are technically classified as markerless AR, in that they do not require physical markers to activate digital content.

Location-based AR

Location-based AR ties digital content and the experience it creates to a specific location. Objects are mapped and appear on the screen when the user's location matches a predetermined location.

I don't believe this is what Mom had in mind when she said, "Go outdoors and have some fun. "Pokémon Go, the game that brought augmented reality to the masses, is an example of location-based AR. In this experience, virtual Pokémon appear in our world through our smartphones, and users are encouraged to find as many of the characters as possible.

Projection-based AR

Projected AR is a little different from other markerless AR. That is, it does not require a mobile device to display the content. Instead, it uses light to project digital graphics onto objects and surfaces, providing users with an interactive experience.

That's right, holograms! Projected AR is used to create 3D objects that can be interactively manipulated by the user. Prototypes and mock-ups of new products can be displayed, and even each part can be disassembled to show the internal structure.

Autlining AR

AR delineation recognizes and assists with boundaries and lines that are unrecognizable to the human eye. Augmented reality rendering uses object recognition to understand the user's immediate environment. Think of driving in low-light conditions or looking at the structure of a building from the outside.

Recognition-based AR

For example, when you read a barcode or QR code on your cell phone, you are actually using object recognition technology. In fact, except for location-based AR, we are using some kind of recognition system to detect the object to be augmented.

Recognition-based AR technologies are also used in various applications: one is to detect an object in front of the camera and provide information about that object on the screen. This is somewhat similar to AR applications for travelers (location navigation). However, the difference is that AR location navigation usually does not know about the object it is looking at, while recognition-based AR applications do.

Item recognition

Refers to the ability to identify the shape, form, and spatial location of various objects captured by the device's camera. Augmented reality is an extension of the real world view by overlaying graphics, text, video, audio, and other computer graphics, and all AR applications are severely challenged, especially object recognition. Most of these applications are marker-rich, using photos, images, and special objects to trigger predefined 3D visualizations, animations, videos, and soundtracks. In other words, they detect and track objects to determine what relevant information should be added to the real world.

Industries reaping augmented reality

Augmented reality is having a huge impact on our daily lives. While augmented reality has its roots in entertainment and games like Snapchat filters and Pokemon Go, AR technology is growing. Today, nearly every industry, from healthcare to manufacturing, is waking up to the potential of AR to provide business solutions that would have been unthinkable a few years ago. Here are some fascinating augmented reality examples of how this technology is changing the way we do business.

Manufacturing

In an industry like manufacturing, there is no room for even a single mistake in the development process. The slightest mistake becomes a reason to rework or improve an existing product, which is costly and time consuming.

Augmented reality provides an excellent solution to easily detect manufacturing errors. With the ability to 3D scan product prototypes, this technology makes prototypes easy to access and understand. Business leaders can easily make the right decisions and teams can act effectively. This increases the speed and efficiency of the process, ultimately creating a better overall experience and benefit.

Healthcare

AR technology is having a disruptive impact on the world of healthcare by breaking complex medical concepts into interactive 3D forms.

In this way, AR is helping healthcare professionals more easily explain diseases and treatments to patients and trainees. By viewing organs in 3D from different angles, surgeons can perform more precise sutures and increase their success rate.

Education

AR technology is changing the verticals of the education business in two ways: by engaging users and making concepts interactive.

By bringing a gaming element into the classroom, AR provides a special experience for both teachers and students.

It turns a boring lesson into a phenomenal experience and makes it easy to learn complex concepts with 3D AR modeling. They can learn beyond the textbook and satisfy their curiosity.

In addition, tutors and teachers can provide the right environment for students to produce their best results. For example, by turning a classroom into an augmented reality playground or a high-resolution gym, physical education teachers can easily encourage students to actively practice.

Ar-based stores, signage, posters, flyers, brochures, t-shirts, etc.

AR brings previously static marketing media to life: storefronts, brochures, posters, t-shirts, flyers, posters, etc. Using AR you can include 3D animations, videos, and targeting information.

This way you can provide your target audience with an informative and seamless experience.

Fashion and Beauty

Augmented reality is transforming the beauty industry by providing customers with virtual assistance to try on the latest fashions and cosmetics from the comfort of their own home.

For example, department store chain Macy's is helping to simplify the cosmetics selection process for customers who want to try beauty products without standing in long lines at the counter.

Using AR technology, the company has created a mobile app that allows users to choose from thousands of beauty products and shades and get a personalized makeover.

This way, shoppers can get an idea of what they want before they even set foot in the store.

Dining

Augmented reality bridges the gap between the consumer, the product, and the product's content.

AR can, for example, make it easier for the end consumer to get detailed information about ingredients and nutritional values at a restaurant. As a result, chefs can be encouraged to experiment and create new recipes that consumers will want to consume.

Applications of augmented reality

According to a recent report by Marketsandmarkets, the augmented reality market is estimated to grow to $72.7 billion by 2024, showing an upward trend. This is because companies and universities are interested in investing in applications that support the still unexplored concept of augmented reality Would you like to know a little more about the applications that extend the capabilities of AR? Let's find out a little more about some of the most practical modern applications for a true representation of the digital world.

Using AR glasses

AR smart glasses are a type of wearable transparent device. They come in a variety of designs, sizes and shapes, but all contribute to a common goal: an enhanced reality: since 2017, the AR smart glasses market has accounted for a compound annual growth rate of 13% for each type of monocular or binocular [according to a MARKET Research Future evaluation report].

The main reason for this increased demand is that these glasses combine virtual information (3D images, animations, videos, etc.) with real-world scenes and bring them into the field of view of users of different ages. examples of smart glasses used for augmented reality in 2021 include Google Glass Enterprise Edition 2, Microsoft HoloLens 2, Oculus Quest 2, Raptor AR Headset, and Magic Leap One. All of these overlay digital information on real objects, allowing users to track emails and texts, and access important details about their rotation. However, if users feel the need to adapt to a different working environment, any AR glasses (of their choice) can be robustly redesigned to project a high-quality color screen in front of them, without compromising on the quality of the display.

AR in the medical field

AR has successfully provided a number of approaches to deal with the complex medical situations of patients and to organize the data of various surgeries. In this way, it can provide powerful support to the general public in providing proper treatment that relaxes the mind and flushes out all the toxins in the body. Medical imaging is an example of augmented reality in the medical industry.. This is done by surgeons, neurologists, chemotherapists, and others to better examine parts of the patient's body for medical effectiveness, and there are many different types of diagnoses. Such parts include the brain, ears, heart, and lungs. You may be wondering how medical professionals perform such diagnosis.

They use AR applications to determine the terminal structures, margins, or morphology of diseases such as tumors and cancers. These apps then provide relevant insights after infiltrating the patient's body in an interactive, augmented 3-D format. This could make intermediate or poor survival surgeries not only safer, but also more accurate. This is because doctors and chemotherapists can now see inside the patient to predict the probability of disease development and to accurately assess the patient's condition. Then, based on the data presented by the AR application, such as graphs and images of the hospitalized patient's body parts, the specialist will be able to perform the appropriate medical treatment.

Enjoying AR on mobile phones

AR has pushed the current limits of cell phones to the point where we can now see things we have wondered and wondered about for centuries as a reality. Measuring the height and width of a kitchen table, designing environments that interest real-world entities like various pieces of furniture, all of this is made possible by mobile applications using augmented reality technology. 2021's most famous

AR-based mobile app is the " The most famous AR-based mobile app in 2021 is the "Ruler App" (5 million downloads Plus), which is available for Android, iPad, and iPhone and can be used as an on-screen ruler tool to measure the dimensions of entities such as sofas, cushions, tables, and vases in real time.

Dimensions are measured in linear sizes such as meters, millimeters, centimeters, inches, yards, and feet, without compromising the accuracy of the surface recognized by the phone's camera. Besides dimension recognition, there are other mobile apps such as DecorateAR, Dulux Visualizer, Paint Tester, etc., which use augmented reality technology to generate home decorating ideas such as furniture placement, resizing of various home entities according to the context of the home environment, etc. This allows you to accurately estimate the materials needed for home decoration, virtually cover walls, and flexibly generate high-resolution views in seconds.

AR is well integrated with the entertainment industry

The entertainment industry in 2021 sees AR as a considerable marketing opportunity because it allows entertainment brands to successfully integrate their branded content with the characters that audiences love the most. These characters can be revolutionary, analytical, idealistic, or humorous, depending on the level of interest shown by the audience in real time. There are a number of entertainment apps that use augmented reality technology models, some of the best known include Snapchat, Google Lens, and Augment. Each of these apps allows you to curate your entertainment with easy-to-use view filters, stickers, lenses, and emoticons.

All of these options allow you to positively express the moments you share with family and friends. Also, entertainment industry experts in 2021 believe that these entertainment apps will incorporate chronological stories to make entertainment much more realistic. Whether you are traveling or watching a comedy show, you can create content anytime, anywhere and successfully integrate it into your marketing campaigns. What we need to be aware of when creating content is that it is real-time object-oriented. If you don't pay enough attention to that, it will negatively affect their tagline of spreading awareness of a product that has yet to be discovered for its merits by premium user accounts.

Travel-n-tourism's ar is now open

Travel-n-Tourism is all about managing clients and travelers as they explore every corner of their destination with accommodation arranged by travel agents and tour operators. However, if travel services are not delivered to customers on time, it can dramatically slow down the growth of revenue generated by travel agencies. That's why travel agents and hotels are introducing AR-based travel apps to help people explore their destinations without compromising on the quality of transportation or food. Some of the augmented reality travel apps used by travel agents and hotels include World Around Me, Smartify, ViewRanger and AR City.

Whether you're struggling to locate transportation, gas stations, ATMs or temples, or you're excited to scan the brochures of agents and travel agencies offering affordable accommodations, any of these apps can help you identify what you're really looking for. Thanks to these augmented reality-based apps, all the details you need about the itinerary, the modes of transportation you may be familiar with, and some hotel accommodations you booked after narrowing down your options are included. Now you can experience the local attractions near your destination without leaving your bed.

AR in education in the classroom

Augmented Reality is actively working with teachers, university professors and other educators to ensure that students of all ages are able to deeply absorb the learning of subjects included in the curriculum. The subjects can be related to science, math, music, psychology, etc. and their concepts can be fully explained at low cost since AR technology does not require any infrastructure. Anytime, anywhere, without additional equipment, students can use Mondly (AR language assistant) to learn new languages, such as German, Spanish or French.

And, if you want to explore the volcanoes and sandstorms of Earth's geological landmarks in a fun and engaging way, Google Earth (an AR-based application) gives students the ability to search, zoom, rotate or tilt the 3D landscape around the Earth. In addition, students can access a larger collection of images, including aerial photographs, street views, and satellite imagery. These apps that support augmented reality are compatible with various versions of Android and iOS, allowing teachers to impart knowledge seamlessly and students to enrich their learning experience with less effort.

Thus, students (or even children) will never fail to have access to such freedom while learning. This allows them to effectively manage their time and hone their skills through such a profitable and augmented digital platform.

AR for public safety

Public safety is about protecting the public from disasters, crimes and other unknown dangers. Whether you work in customer service or in a drug control agency, safety is something that cannot be compromised. the app developers at KOVA corp understand this and, as a result, capture photos and videos of unexpected events such as instant and safe disasters from your smartphone The result is Silent Partner, an AR-based app that captures photos and videos of unexpected events such as instant and safe disasters from your smartphone.

The app allows users to take photos and videos with their smartphones in the event of a disaster or other unforeseen event, and later send the videos and photos to themselves (or to a public safety officer or police officer) for easy geotagging and retrieval anywhere. The app also has a voice analysis function, which can inform investigators about voice content to ensure citizen safety.

In addition, an AR app for drivers (iOnRoad Augmented Driving Lite App) uses the smartphone's GPS, sensors and native camera to detect vehicles and warn the driver before the vehicle crashes. In the unlikely event that the driver misses notification of a collision, an audible warning appears to direct the driver to apply the brakes or slow the vehicle so that it can arrive safely and on time at a predefined location. Such applications act as a powerful aid to responsible citizens involved with driving companies and the police, as they will think less about plans that are not appropriate from a public safety perspective.

Car manufacturers are also getting involved in AR

Porsche is experimenting with AR as a new way to assist mechanics in servicing and maintaining the "pride and joy" of its customers.

Its "Tech Live Look" allows Porsche's remote service engineers to connect to Porsche's headquarters in Atlanta using ODG smart augmented reality glasses to receive real-time assistance.

Porsche mechanics can direct remote staff to work with live guides, video tutorials, documentation, and other pertinent information.

The idea is to improve the efficiency of repairs and also help speed up customer service.

Harley-Davidson is using AR to help customers in-store

The retail sector is also starting to use AR to help customers have a more enjoyable and interactive shopping experience.

Shoppers have been using their smartphones to compare prices and get information about products in-store for some time, but Harley-Davidson has taken this to the next level by integrating AR.

They have developed a special app that allows customers to see the bike in the store and customize it (change the paint, add accessories) using their cell phones.

This is an interesting AR application and one that will become equally common in other big brands such as Ikea. Several apps have also been developed that use AR to allow customers to remotely "try on" items before buying them online.

AR for f-35 helmets

The F-35 is not only a very expensive fighter jet, but one pilot's helmet costs only 400,000 yen.

These helmets are designed to allow AR features, such as real-time video from the fighter's external cameras, to be overlaid directly on the pilot's field of view.

This system allows the pilot to have a 360-degree view of the surroundings of his aircraft, eliminating blind spots. The pilot can also zoom in on areas of interest, and if a potential threat is detected, he can attack it with his plane.

It also provides pilots with "digital night vision," a virtual HUD, weapon system information, and targeting system capabilities, with the ability to add new features in the future.

AR is increasingly being used in tv broadcasting

From weather forecasts to sports broadcasts, AR is becoming commonplace in television. AR is ideal for these applications and can make a subject come alive for the general public.

AR can be used in educational documentaries, sports broadcasts, and other news programs to help people understand more esoteric subjects. A good example of this is the BBC's coverage of the general election.

Such AR applications are immersive and engaging.

Gatwick airport aids gate search with AR

Augmented reality is being used in an app at Gatwick Airport to help passengers board planes. Their app has been so successful that it has recently won an award as well.

The app won the National Technology Awards' Mobile Innovation of the Year Award in 2017. It provides passengers with personalized airport locations and plans to integrate intelligent chatbots to further improve the service.

The app uses more than 2,000 beacons to guide passengers through the terminal with an AR-based map on their smartphones, covering two busy terminals. Once this app matures, it is expected to greatly improve the overall traffic flow in the airport.

AR is ideal for interior design and modeling

So it's no surprise that it has applications in architectural design and construction. AR can help professionals easily visualize the final project during the planning phase.

They can even take a virtual tour of the project using headphones and tinker with the project in a fully immersive experience. This can also be applied to urban planners, who can model and tour an entire city layout.

AR is perfect for any activity that has a spatial design component.

Mixed Reality

MR is a blend of real world and digital elements. Mixed Reality uses next generation sensing and imaging technologies to manipulate and interact with objects and environments, both physical and virtual. Mixed Reality allows you to immerse yourself in the world around you while wearing a headset and manipulating the virtual environment with your bare hands. It is as if you have one foot (or hand) in the real world and the other in the imaginary one. It removes the basic concept between reality and fantasy and provides an experience that will change the way we play and work today.

Extended Reality

Extended Reality (XR) is a universal term that includes the immersive learning technologies VR (Virtual Reality), AR (Augmented Reality), and MR (Mixed Reality). These technologies augment reality by adding value to or simulating the real world through digital learning materials, and have become an effective means of modernizing corporate training programs.

Incorporating XR into training can immerse students in a multisensory environment that is more interactive, engaging, and effective in the long run.

Pros and cons of extended reality

Pros of Extended Reality

- Enables safe experiential learning - XR training creates a safe training space for experiential learning where learners can take risks, practice, and learn from their mistakes.
- Realistic practice of hard and soft skills - XR technology allows learners to develop hard skills (such as operating and repairing equipment) and soft skills (such as communication and empathy) through

realistic interactions with people and equipment.

- Convenient extension and reuse - With XRS and additional access options, organizations can conveniently extend XR training across the organization and reuse the content as much as needed.
- Collection of key metrics to help determine ROI - XRS collects key training metrics that measure knowledge retention and helps indicate whether the investment has a measurable ROI.

Cons of Extended Reality

- High initial development and equipment costs - Since XR is a new technology in the training arena, the initial development and equipment costs can be higher compared to traditional learning methods.
- Solutions - Some ways to mitigate the cost of XR training include starting with a pilot program, using in-house resources and staff, etc.
- Health risks and side effects - AR and VR technologies can pose certain health risks to learners, such as nausea, headaches, and eye strain.
- Solutions - To avoid potential health risks and safety hazards, organizations need to

provide alternative ways to access training. For example, learners who are not comfortable wearing a headset can access XR training from their desktops.

- Technology Advancements and Irregular Updates - Like any modern technology, XR is subject to irregular updates in hardware and software.
- Solution - Investing in XRS makes it easy to deliver the latest content regardless of where your students are located; XRS eliminates the need to move around or move equipment every time content is updated.

Security and privacy issues in augmented reality

One of the biggest perceived dangers of augmented reality relates to privacy: AR technology can see what the user is doing, which puts the user's privacy at risk. AR collects far more information about who the user is and what they are doing than, for example, social media networks or other technologies. This raises concerns and questions.

If a hacker gains access to the device, the potential for loss of privacy is very great.

How do AR companies use and protect the information they collect from users?

Where do companies store augmented reality data? Will it be stored locally on the device or will it be stored in the cloud? If sent to the cloud, is the information encrypted?

Will the AR company share this data with third parties? If so, how are they using it?

Untrustworthy Content

AR browsers facilitate the process of augmentation, but the content is created and distributed by third-party vendors and apps. This is problematic because AR is a relatively new area and the mechanisms for generating and transmitting authenticated content have not yet evolved, making it untrustworthy. Sophisticated hackers can replace a user's AR with their own by tricking the user or providing false information.

Various cyber threats can make content untrustworthy, even if the source is authentic. Spoofing, sniffing, and data manipulation are examples of these techniques.

Social Engineering

Due to the potentially unreliable nature of the content, augmented reality systems can be an effective tool to trick users as part of a social engineering attack. For example, hackers can distort a user's perception of reality through fake signs and displays to trick them into acting in their favor.

Malware

AR hackers can embed malicious content into applications through advertisements. Clicking on an ad can compromise the security of your AR by directing you to a hostage-taking website or an AR server infected with malware and displaying unreliable images.

Theft Of Network Credentials

Criminals may be able to steal network credentials from Android-powered handheld devices. For retailers using augmented or virtual reality shopping apps, hacking can pose a cyber-threat. Many customers already have their card details and mobile payment methods recorded in their user profiles. Since mobile payments are a very simple procedure, hackers could gain access to these and quietly drain the account.

Denial Of Service

Another possible security attack against ARs is denial of service. For example, users who use ARs for their business could find themselves suddenly cut off from the flow of information they are receiving. Especially for professionals who use ARs in critical situations, not being able to access information can have serious consequences. For example, a surgeon may suddenly lose access to important real-time information through his AR glasses, or a driver may suddenly find that his AR windshield turns into a black screen and he can't see the road.

Man-In-The-Middle Attack

In order to eavesdrop on communication between an AR browser and an AR provider, AR channel owner, or third-party server, the attacker must be located on the network. Man-in-the-middle attacks are possible as a result of this situation

Ransomware

Hackers can gain access to a user's augmented reality device and record the user's actions and interactions in an AR environment. They can then threaten to release these recordings unless the user pays a ransom. This can be embarrassing and distressing for individuals who do not want their games or other AR interactions made public.

Physical Damage

One of the most significant security vulnerabilities of wearable AR devices is physical damage. While some wearable devices are more durable than others, physical vulnerabilities exist in all devices. Maintaining functionality and security is an essential part of ensuring safety-for example, ensuring that headphones, which can be easily lost or stolen, are not removed.

The dangers and safety issues of virtual reality

The security threats of VR are slightly different from AR, as VR is limited to an enclosed environment and involves no interaction with the real physical world. However, since VR headsets cover the user's entire field of view, they can be dangerous if hackers take over the device. For example, it is possible to manipulate the content in such a way as to make the user dizzy or nauseous.

VR Concerns

As with AR, privacy is a major concern in VR: a key privacy issue in VR is that the data collected-biometric data such as iris and retina, finger and palm prints, facial geometry, and voice prints-is highly personal. For example, there are

- **Fingerprint Tracking**

In a virtual world, a user can use hand gestures in the same way as in the real world. For example, they might use their finger to type a code on a virtual keyboard. However, this would result in finger tracking data being recorded and transmitted to the system, indicating that the finger entered a

PIN. If an attacker can retrieve this data, they can recreate the user's PIN.

- **Eye Tracking**

Some VR and AR headsets have eye tracking. Malicious actors may be able to gain additional benefit from this information. By knowing exactly what the user is looking at, an attacker could obtain valuable information that could be captured and used to recreate the user's behavior.

It is nearly impossible to anonymize VR and AR tracking data due to the unique behavioral patterns of individuals; using the behavioral and biological information collected by VR headsets, researchers were able to identify users with a very high degree of accuracy.

Like zip codes, IP addresses, and voiceprints, VR and AR tracking data should be considered potential "personally identifiable information" (PII). It can be considered PII because other parties may use it, alone or in combination with other personal or identifying information, to distinguish or track the identity of an individual. Therefore, VR privacy has become a major concern.

Ransomware

Attackers can also inject features into the VR platform to trick users into providing personal information. similar to AR, ransomware attacks can be used by malicious parties to destroy the platform and demand a ransom.

Fake Ids, Or "Deep Fakes

Machine learning technology can process audio and video to the extent that it looks like real video. If a hacker has access to the motion tracking data of a VR headset, they could use it to create a digital replica (sometimes called a deep fake), making VR less secure. This can then be superimposed on other people's VR experiences to create social engineering attacks.

The biggest danger of virtual reality, not only for cyber security, is that it completely cuts off the user's visual and auditory connection to the outside world. It is always important to assess the physical security and safety of the user environment first. This is also true for AR, especially in immersive environments, where users need to be very aware of their surroundings.

Other Issues With V.R That Critics Sometimes Describe As Negatives Of Virtual Reality Are As Follows

- Possibility of addiction.
- Health effects - Dizziness, nausea, loss of spatial awareness, etc. (after prolonged VR use).
- Loss of connection with people.

Examples of AR and VR

The applications of augmented reality, virtual reality, and mixed reality are diverse and expanding. They include the following

Gaming - From FPS to strategy games to role-playing adventures, the most famous AR game is probably Pokémon Go.

Professional sports - for training programs that support both professional and amateur athletes.

Virtual travel - such as virtual trips to zoos, safari parks, museums and other attractions. - All from the comfort of your home.

Healthcare - Enables training for medical professionals, such as simulating surgery.

Movies and TV - For a more enhanced experience in movies and shows.

This technology is also being used in more serious fields. For example, the U.S. Army is using it to digitally enhance soldiers' training missions, and in China, police are using it to identify suspects.

Privacy concerns with Oculus

Oculus is one of the best-known VR headsets and one of the few that supports large-scale VR game development; Facebook acquired the company in 2014, and in 2020 Facebook announced that it will require Facebook login for future VR headsets. Oculus is one of the few products that support development. This development sparked a heated debate about Oculus' privacy.

Criticisms of the decision concern the way Facebook collects, stores, and uses data and the potential for ad targeting, as well as being forced to use services they might not have otherwise chosen to use. The announcement has led to a number of comments online from users who are concerned about Oculus' security and that they will no longer use Oculus headsets, but commenters seem to feel that this will not hinder Oculus in the long run.

Tips: ensuring safety when using VR and AR systems

- Avoid disclosing information that is too personal.

Do not disclose information that is too personal or that does not need to be disclosed. Creating an account via email is one way to do this, but do not create a credit card unless you are explicitly purchasing something.

- Review your privacy policy.

It's easy to overlook lengthy privacy policies and terms of service. However, it's worth trying to find out how the companies behind AR and VR platforms store your data and how they handle it. For instance, are they disclosing your information to third parties? What kind of data are they sharing or collecting?

- Use a VPN.

One way to keep your personal information and data private on the web is to use a VPN service. If you need to disclose sensitive information, using a VPN can help prevent that information from being compromised. Advanced encryption and modified IP addresses work in tandem to protect your personal information and data, and with the development of AR and VR, the VPN model is likely to expand in these technological realities.

- Keep your firmware up to date

It is important to keep the firmware of your VR or AR headset up to date. In addiction to adding new features and improving existing ones, updates can also fix security flaws.

- Use comprehensive anti-virus software

In general, the best way to stay safe online is to use a proactive cybersecurity solution. Kaspersky Total Security offers powerful protection against a wide range of online threats. These include viruses, malware, ransomware, spyware, phishing and other emerging Internet security threats.

CONCLUSION

As for what metric investors should look for Metaverse-related coins, Grayscale's Maximo says it's "hard to say" because most coins in the Metaverse and gaming world are outside the top 100.

Since it's early, he said, investors should look at the usual metrics-market capitalization, transaction volume, number of transactions, protocol revenue-but it's better to think on a thematic level and bet on whether the infrastructure or a particular game will catch on.

"The number of transactions and protocol revenues indicate the number of users and the frequency of their interactions with the game. These metrics help us understand the market capitalization and trade volume of tokens associated with a project and can color in which direction a token is likely to trade," Maximo says.

He adds, "You also need to do your due diligence on these categories." "It's such an early ecosystem, most have market capitalizations of less than $1 billion, and they are very volatile, so a lot of research is needed."

Building Wealth

He added that Axie Infinity and Sandbox seem to be the most promising projects out there in terms of market capitalization, marketing and community building.

In the gaming world, one of the key metrics that investors should be looking at is community building, which Maximo says is a difficult metric to track.

So the easiest way to do it is to look at how games are doing on social media, particularly YouTube and Twitter, where gamers interact with game developers and content creators the most. Game videos and livestreams are an important way to bring new players into the game.

And that's just the beginning.

As many experts point out, we are only at the beginning of what the Metaverse has to offer, and the investment opportunities will continue to grow.

Tobias Batton, CEO and founder of publisher Ex Populus, told GOBankingRates that video games have historically provided people with a small sample of what the Metaverse has to offer in terms of community building, virtual markets, and cross-cultural relationships in a shared virtual environment. " Recent technological advancements, on the other hand, have provided humanity only a small sampling of what the Metaverse has to offer

However, with recent technological developments, the potential utility of the Metaverse is limitless.

Investors looking to invest in a truly transformative crypto project should look beyond the idea that the Metaverse is a "virtual world," he added.

"The Metaverse is a framework for connectivity, and has cross-sectoral utility, from energy to reforestation and environmental solutions, to gaming and new immersive forms of digital interaction, allowing users to use their accumulated digital assets in new and functional ways," he shared.

How Can We, The Commoners, Participate?

What's remarkable about the crypto-based Metaverse project is that one can acquire resources and tangible assets within the Metaverse and exchange them for other digital and real-world assets," says San Morales, Chief Operating Officer of Myobu, a new GameFi project from Spain. (It's the intersection of gaming and finance. There are already several blockchain projects that make it possible to make a living simply by playing games. Think Axie Infinity (AXS), for example," he says, talking about Sky Mavis' Vietnam-based blockchain game, where you can make "money" with NFTs and sell it with fiat.

We are now creating a parallel universe, folks

Myobu started as a community token in June 2021 and we have now started working on creating games for the Metaverse. They plan to release it in stages on the blockchain, starting with a fairly simple card game and moving into an immersive, full-fledged role-playing game in the later stages. The cards are available from Uniswap.

Roman Nekrasov, a serial IT entrepreneur from Russia and co-founder of the ENCRY Foundation, believes that the creation of Metaverse will act as a catalyst for the development of blockchain systems for decentralized governance, decentralized finance and smart contracts in general.

He cites buying the foundation's builders as another way for investors to get into the Metaverse.

"Think Ethereum (ETH), Polka Dot (DOT), Solana (SOL), Cardano (ADA)," he says. Not only are "blockchain systems for creating decentralized applications" important, but also infrastructure-building blockchain projects that are created for seamless passing between blockchains. I think Polkadot is a notable example of this." Polkadot hopes to solve a very important challenge: ensuring interoperability between multiple blockchains within a single platform. Seamless sending and receiving between blockchains will be a necessity in the near future. In the next five years, Polkadot will... I think we have a bright future ahead of us."

Mister Discus Fish agrees.

He says, "The first step is to invest in the infrastructure of the Metaverse platform and ecosystem." In general, the token economy underlying the ecosystem is a commons investment. The other is to invest in core NFT assets on (specific) Metaverse platforms. The third way is to invest in social tokens, because social interaction in the Metaverse is the most important aspect of the NFT. The third way is to invest in social tokens, because social interaction in the Metaverse can bring about several new social networking applications and create a fan economy.

Social tokens are a sort of cryptocurrency that is based on a community, influencer, or brand as its central focus. They can be part of the Metaverse or unrelated to the Metaverse. It's another way to diversify your crypto portfolio beyond just owning Bitcoin, Ethereum, and classic alts like Filecoin and Litecoin.

Yanpolskiy, who this year ranked as one of the blockchain influencers to follow on Hackernoon, said, "It's crazy what you see out there in terms of the development of their community. They're now building a multi-billion dollar, player-controlled gaming ecosystem.

With the idea of gamifying the entire token ecosystem, Yanpolskiy has created his own play-to-earn gaming guild, CGU.io." Play to win: the Metaverse is calling," he says on his website, which looks like a cross between a pink flying pig, a lamb and a chicken. It has its own chip (CGU is the ticker), which trades for around $2.

According to Yanpolskiy, Crypto Gaming United currently has 70,000 members in about 26 countries. In case you're interested, here's how to follow them on Instagram.

I would rather invest than play. Virtual worlds like this one seem like a complete waste of time, check out The Sandbox. This Minecraft-like game has its own symbol, "SAND." It started out with a value of $0.03. Now, with a price of $2.7, it appears that about $2 billion has been invested in this token.

"Buy virtual land or assets and start developing them," said Joel Dietz, formerly of ArtWallet and a founding member of Ethereum." Diversify your bets by joining a hundred or so projects with growth potential."

Dietz is behind Metaverse, a new platform for building the Metaverse, which began in late October." We've only recently begun offering our own land sales as a result of the high level of interest generated by Dubai Blockchain Week," the company announced through its press office, which closed on October 18.

Today's investors are likely to be "Metaverse gurus". The Metaverse now has the potential to take "The Sims" to a whole new level. We are creating a parallel system of existence that will change exactly how we live, how we interact with the rest of the world, and how we do business. In other words, we may be able to hire someone in the Metaverse. So, in the new dystopia, what did you do wrong that got you fired? Create a parallel world in the Metaverse and make a living from it. That's what's going to happen. This was pre-Star Wars.

Facebook is said to be hiring 10,000 people in the EU to develop the Zuck Metaverse on its Horizon World platform, according to Nigel Green, CEO and founder of asset management firm deVere Group.

"Facebook's statement reaffirms that stakeholders do not regard the Metaverse as a 'extension' of the Internet, but rather as its successor," argues Green

As a side note, and this is not exactly due to the Metaverse, but due to crypto, Grayscale's total assets under management now exceed $60 billion, which is larger than State Street's STT +1.9% Gold ETF (GLD) GLD +0. This is larger than the 2%. Grayscale started launching crypto ETFs around 2017; the SPDR Gold fund has been around since 2004.

The Metaverse is a unique place where the physical world and the digital world come together. It is a future that has been predicted in many science fiction books and movies over the years, but this future has finally arrived.

Even though the Metaverse market is still in its early stages, it has great potential and will transform the tech industry in just a couple of years. So, don't wait for tomorrow and regret it, join this trend today!

"Thank you for reading this book. If you enjoyed it, and if you want, please visit the site where you purchased it and leave a brief review.

Your feedback is important to me and will help other readers decide whether to read the book too.

Thank You!"

Darell Freeman

Cryptosphere Academy

www.ingramcontent.com/pod-product-compliance
Ingram Content Group UK Ltd.
Pitfield, Milton Keynes, MK11 3LW, UK
UKHW040007200726
13854UKWH00001B/94

9 798201 451059